T0064725

Black Caps and Red Feathers

And

Ancestral Earth

(Two Plays)

John Nkemngong Nkengasong

Langaa Research & Publishing CIG
Mankon, Bamenda

Publisher:
Langaa RPCIG
Langaa Research & Publishing Common Initiative Group
P.O. Box 902 Mankon
Bamenda
North West Region
Cameroon
Langaagrp@gmail.com
www.langaa-rpcig.net

Distributed outside N. America by African Books Collective
orders@africanbookscollective.com
www.africanbookcollective.com

Distributed in N. America by Michigan State University Press
msupress@msu.edu
www.msupress.msu.edu

ISBN: 9956-578-38-X

© John Nkemngong Nkengasong 2010

For
Cameroonians
who survive
by the compassion of the garbage heap
- for shelter, food, clothing, etc.

Table of Contents

Introduction

The two plays in this publication, *Black Caps and Red Feathers* and *Ancestral Earth*, have an ancestry of works that challenge traditional postcolonial binaries, given the fluid boundaries of Cameroon's postcoloniality. This distinction is necessary in order to better appraise the complex nature of overlapping concepts that Anglophone Cameroon literature in particular encompasses. Our culturally relative encounters with art in general become even more demanding in any assessment of what is simplified as 'Cameroon literature' because of the country's unique postcolonial identity into which sister analyses of say the Canadian example cannot quite fit. Nkengasong's works fall within this amoebic space and problematise the very notions of identity, belonging, and self/collective responsibility that are flagged in postcolonial discussions.

In-between the two plays here, we have a subtly articulated *The Call of Blood* that couches the cultural, ideological, and sectarian vibrations that we experience before and after it in a personalised and domesticated invocation of mystical fantasising after the allure of power and its consequences. The play unravels similar conspiracies of a status coterie within the Country's People Democratic Murderers party as in *The Widow's Might*, and therefore circumvents public spaces and their advertised ideologies into Efenze's private horrors that recur with a hellish nuisance. Vengeance becomes the site for the vicious circle around which 'the call of blood' is enacted. Although madness is not directly the consequence of political manoeuvres, Efenze and Manka's eventual migration to the garbage heap fulfils the retributive strategy that the play maps out from sentiments that bracket Lady Macbeth's calculating brutality in *Macbeth* with Sartre's refraction of hell-in-life or otherwise, in *No Exit*. With this 'limitation', I find it very convenient, therefore, to read *Ancestral Earth* as the sequel to, if not the flipside of *Black Caps and Red Feathers* with a causal thematisation of bleakness and hope. The common denominator in both plays is communal grudge against irresponsible leadership and its fallouts of indiscriminate victimization that allow for the anticipation of a new or renewed consciousness.

Black Caps and Red Feathers is an acutely pathetic enactment of contingent Cameroon and her leaders as they confront and try to circumvent the inevitability of history – Truth – revisiting them. It is a scary play whose even more scary characters in their abstractness epitomise the enthronement of bastardom as political logic. Creature, the main character, with a rather over-deterministic will, provides the uncensored medium through which the shameless betrayal of the clan and its citizens is revealed. As a significant representative of people whose 'tongues are barbarous' to the halo of political convenience in the clan, Creature is the characteristic political prisoner who has been abused in detention into insanity. His life now, as a 'free' man, is a long reverie of pain and horror, as he recalls every second of his incarceration, the inhuman cruelty against him that has been trivialised into popular normalcy, and from which even a prophet (as the quasi-Greek Chorus character, Lunatic, calls him) can emerge, broken. His words are the archetypal ranting of Everyman whose collective unconscious is the implicating realm of woe, rot and obnoxious cannibalism. And even then, Creature still targets the blunt claws of such tyranny that ends up ruining its own potentials through a sadistic insistence on collective submission.

In the confrontation, a pro-socialist vision is pitted against the negating hangover of imperialism, recalling the nationalist uprising of the 1960s when militants of the *Union des Populations du Cameroun*, UPCists, challenged the infected foundations of the neophyte nation. In the play, as a consequence, Womba '[faces] a butcher squad because he had turned terrorist when he was [only] out to save the clan'; while on his part Ganje 'wanted to see the people's green lawns, their green fields and rubbish heaps swell out fruits for the people themselves'. The line between history and art is therefore a very thin one in the play and in this way it attempts a redefinition of Cameroon's national image as a justification, for and/or against those who partook in shading its changing cycle.

It is in this way too that the play fits within the emerging context of Cameroon Anglophone Drama, to meaningfully vindicate opponents of a Bjornson generalisation against the impact of this *localised* genre. For, from Musinga to Nkengasong the picture becomes clearer with each new play that is placed on the shelves, and more focused in ascertaining the fertility of such a phenomenon that does not seek to flatter incumbency with Chococam-coated phrases. The consciousness is unique and interestingly so against the cookies of epicurean fallacy, in its strident estimation of what was, and of what is supposed to be, an embracing whole. 'My two countrymen', Creature laments, were 'lured to the other side of the Great River' by the arch tyrant-deceiver, Traourou, 'with throngs of men to betray and cut their heads'. The representative victim is Bobe Khom, and reminiscent of Bate Besong's 'Grain of Bobe Ngom Jua' whose local constituency was the Kom clan in the Anglophone North West Region of Cameroon, the lament is acrimonious: the traitors did not only 'sell' their people, but also 'changed the course of the Great River' (one of them confesses), only to be rewarded with menial jobs: 'They assigned me to wash the latrine and kill cockroaches', the other concurs. In this way, then, Nkengasong is concerned with the signposted mentality of a people, which survives even the crudest form of osmotic stereotyping and vindicates them as it were, in history books as fodder for change. It is a mentality that must survive, of necessity, to tell its own story without gloss, a task that is examined in the novel *Across the Mongolo* by the same author, that deals with the conflicting consciousness of crossing 'the Great River'. The mentality resists imposed definitions and fights to conquer the insinuations of fear in a desperate moment of enslavement, which Creature as lord over his remnant possession regenerates in the significant symbol of fire. This is the hope that never dies even in betrayal, and explains why Creature's heap of rubbish is still vital and coveted. The death of Bobe Khom, then, is just an attempt to kill such hope, after all, since as the personification of 'life', 'history', and 'posterity', his corporeal existence is in fact not necessary for the ultimate realization of the dreams for which he was killed. The rubbish heap metaphor is thus richly ambiguous from both 'national' and 'regional' perspectives and in the latter case in particular, the freedom for which Creature craves is an obsession, which like identity, cannot be bargained.

Desire is therefore a powerful motif in the play, and is dramatically juxtaposed with fear and resistance. The consequences of such desire enrich the irony of the play against the bloating excesses of Traourou and the 'weakling boy' he had groomed as a successor. They have perfected the art of dosing out terror to those who dare to desire the feathered cap of leadership since, ironically, 'to wear the black cap and feather [...] you must use your cuffs on ghosts'. Such raw dictatorship energizes the instinct to breed more fear against real and imaginary opponents. At the same time, those overtly targeted by oppressive brunt of leadership develop resistance tactics that ultimately become lessons for such leadership: 'A king in the clan is supreme but his subjects are more supreme', we are told instructively. And this is where Creature as the custodian of Truth is vulnerable. Apart from conventional threats, he also has to confront and try to overcome, domestic and matrimonial recollections especially when he is expected to ransom his wife, Ngwi, and children, by denouncing the truth for which he stands. And as he concludes with characteristic stoicism that defines his communal symbolism, 'the people can't change their minds even for a million crowns' even if individuals like the two traitors from Shwaart and Mbrouhngwi, do so for thirty pieces of silver.

But the characterisation of leadership in the play is not logical with the unfolding of the plot. The contemporary moment of the play's action is in the aftermath of Traourou's fall from power and it is only his shadow that hangs over the action as a significant backdrop for Creature's rich insanity. But the voice of Traourou's ghost (he had been buried abroad) seeks to impose itself on the present, which is inconsistent with historical fact on which the play itself is patterned. On the whole the latter part of the play, especially with the entrance of Voice, weakens the thematic verve by resorting to, and 'recounting' the raw material of history rather too closely, especially with a shift in tense-use at this point. It is perhaps the inevitable consequence of such drama, yet it taxes the poetry of the earlier part of the play into a colloquial medium of blunt, casual fact.

For all that, however, the inconsistency suggests an absurdly amorphous variety of leadership, which is as blindly nonchalant as it lacks a basic definition of itself and vision. For, in *Black Caps and Red Feathers* is conjured a synonymous picture with Butake's Psaul Roi in *Dance of the Vampires* as victims of corrupt and corruptible power, institutionalised and celebrated as the outrageous landmark of political drudgery. Psaul Roi is the supreme Cause while Creature is the predictable Consequence in a dispensation of antithetical sentiments whose common denominator, nevertheless, is the dismal absurdity of the human endeavour to lead with brute force and resistance to being led as such.

The play ends on an apocalyptic note when Creature swoons and we get these 'blasts of thunder', significantly suggestive of the moment of parturition that should usher in 'some clansman who can count his ancestors from the beginning of time'; and who will then 'lead [a] procession to the ancestral shrine'. It echoes a theme that is increasingly dominant in Cameroon Anglophone literature, namely a movement back to the roots to recognise collective self and re-find identity in a moment of spiritual atonement, 'wailing at ancestral graves' in the hope that 'we might be safe again'. This is the particular achievement of Nkengasong's vision in *Black Caps*, a rallying call for militant introspections into perceptive postures. As Lunatic, the Narrator-Chorus cautions, 'go home and cook your herbs/ get colanuts, palmwine, salt/ swines, goats, njieh, nkeng [...]/ go to Fuandem's shrine/ and in a rite/ weep in the nave till the rocks trembles'.

In *Ancestral Earth* the identified grudge against tyrannical leadership is again communal and rendered (this time) through the women who almost replicate the Chorus in Greek drama – just as Creature recalled the tramps of the Absurdist tradition – and who then wonder 'if this Earth is the same in which our mothers buried our umbilical cords'. It is through these women that we feel the pulse of political and sexual exploitation epitomized by Akeumbin the King. For, in a significant nuancing of themes, even the men in the land are raped into cowardice and submission by the 'native' personification of a neo-colonial nightmare. Drought, disease, and death are the consequences of this situation, with an inscrutable King, 'man beyond man', who 'sits like [...] stones'. Even the Princes who serve as spiritual pillars of the land are now powerless. 'This matter has teeth', one of them confesses, and it is the women who persist in their demands for audience with the King. In doing this, they draw on Ma Kusham's oath of sealed lips in Butake's *Lake God* and then go beyond Mboysiy's lone-soldier militantism in *The Survivors*, and reintroduce Woman as a key partner in the reassessment of a functional leadership.

For people who express such strong emotions against the King in his absence, and yet go on to pour praises on him once he appears on stage, it is possible to conclude that they are also complicit to their destitution, duplicating as it were, mannerisms of hero-worship. However, the need for change from which anger rises also implies that they are disappointed with the recalcitrance of leadership and not with its symbol or personification. It was Victor Epie Ngome who reminded Cameroonians more than two decades ago that a people get the leadership it deserves. This philosophical insight of 'The Rambler' over the then Radio Cameroon explains not just the balkanized polity that is narrated in his allegorical representation of Cameroon, *What God Has Put Asunder*, but also anticipates in a general sense, the nature of Anglophone Cameroon theatre in its specific focus on the ruinous arrogance of leadership. Nkengasong's play, as already suggested, cues in perfectly from this and those of Victor Musinga through Bate Besong and Bole Butake, to depict a gruesome canonization of such a state of tragedy. Akeumbin confesses how, with the assistance of his 'foreign friends' he has 'cut down the forests, and opened the land so that [the people] can work freely on the soil'. This loaded confession translates from the misapplication of globalisation in a political economy that stymies its potential into a dependency status and the best that can be hoped for is a crass, neoliberal 'improvement' on the primary state of the economy. Deforestation becomes the political capital for a leadership that is ignorant of the environmental hazards that attend such gross exploitation, even when the price in human terms confounds any casual observer. And all of this in exchange for trifles such as 'a gun' which is symbolic of the King's oppressive vigour, and 'ornaments' for the King's young wife.

After fifty years of 'flag independence' during which time the postcolonial writer and critic has deciphered every anathema of the globalising world system for a resistance strategy, we are still burdened in *Ancestral Earth* with the retarding evidence of a jumpstarting momentum. At best, it would remain a monotonous hobbling on the same spot, if tyranny is not checked in time. But Akeumbin whose stubbornness pulls the community to the very edge of a precipice, is also vulnerable to both the sensual and plebeian constituencies of his authority, and consequently vacillates between them in a near terminal confrontation with his own sense of invincibility.

The eternal question of the other woman, which almost every strand of feminism glosses over, manifests in this play not in its traditionally antagonistic trajectory, but as an awareness-bringing moment when Afingong exploits her characterisation as the King's Achilles' heel and 'crosses over to join the other [protesting] women'. This decision is a definitive mark in the politics of dualised leadership of male/female components that the play hints at. In his confrontational treaties, *The Anatomy of Female Power*, Chinweizu concedes that men may rule the world, but women rule the men who rule the world. Afingong (whose name is suggestive of a traitor first against the less privileged women and then against the King in order to bring the polarised camps together) justifies Chinweizu's position by rehabilitating Akeumbin, whose phallic imagination (drawing on his own name, perhaps) finally wilts in acknowledgement of people power.

Ancestral Earth thus ends as both a continuation and fulfillment of issues that are raised and suggestively addressed in *Black Caps and Red Feathers*. The ritual demands of the priest in the latter play hope to revive the land in the aftermath of autocratic blunders; but in *Ancestral Earth* there is a necessary cathartic moment on which the past and the present are reconciled. The King's fiftieth wife is the linchpin to this dramatic development, the revived hub of communal consciousness that can no longer be accorded sub-status in the final assessment of cultural mores. While Western-Christian theories of leadership have successfully eclipsed the woman's balancing centrality in this domain, to the extent that even Dan Brown's gnostic and cross-cultural conjectures in *The Da Vinci Code* have been ridiculed by the conservative bloc, it is interesting that *Black Caps and Red Feathers* and *Ancestral Earth* attempt a revival of roots spirituality within a postcolonial space, and how this can be negotiated as a vital intersection with leadership in a deconstruction of Liberation Theology. Identical ritual 'ingredients' in both plays announce – in the second – ancestral voices of a long-awaited renaissance in cultural identification and differentiation that commentators like Franz Fanon and Ali Mazrui had pioneered and popularized respectively as an intertextual crossroads. Even with the overwhelming, and often brutal, force of Capitalist-Christian coercions that target the world's remaining enclaves today, this roots momentum is increasingly becoming a defining characteristic of what I refer to tentatively as postcolonial globalisation, fruitfully reversed for indigenous benefit. Nkengasong's two plays here signal a possible way to ultimate realisation, when leadership will combine male/female and spiritual/secular visions for a more enabling narration of our ever mutating postcolonial context.

Mbuh Tennu
Department of English
University of Yaounde I

Black Caps and Red Feathers

Dramatis Personae

Lunatic
Creature
Voice

The first performance of *Black Caps and Red Feathers* was given on the 1ˢᵗ of July, 1995 in the Catholic Mission Hall Kumba Town by the Royal Spear Theatre Club. It was directed by the author and the cast was as follows:

Creature: Benson Bechemanyor
Lunatic: Denis Ajebesone, who also presented Voice

Echoes of thunder and other noises are heard for a few moments. Silence.
LUNATIC enters, rubbing his eyes. He looks haggard, unkempt and
scared, striding cautiously to the nearest side of the stage; head bowed, stops
and looks up then speaks.)

LUNATIC:
>I had no sleep tonight.
>Even now my heart is crammed with monstrosity,
>with the voices of death and life.
>I had thought to myself
>that I shall tell the story in tears
>when one morning I shall wake from sleep
>to find that I am dead,
>believing that we men who wear our cloaks
>the right sides are sane and civilised men.
>
>But the wailing voices of future generations
>filled my mind
>and peals of thunder rumbled in my heart,
>and I felt Fuandem's wrath
>in his stormy voice that spoke:
>"You Messenger of Truth!
>You are the divine bat that sees all in a dream!
>I sent you to the world to prophesy,
>to fill the lives of men with Truth;
>now you lie there musing,
>feeding on your own thoughts
>like the hen that ate its own eggs.
>How can you, knowing all that is true,
>disdain till after you were dead?
>Glory is he who perceives and speaks it plain;
>or he becomes the snake that refused fewer legs
>because it claimed it was bigger than the millipede
>and died having none."
>
>That is why I came to you, clansmen,
>soon as I saw the first crack of dawn,

to make you see the truth about our fates
Here at life's farthest end *(Pointing towards the stage)*
is death in life,
a Creature of its own kind,
desolate
on the garbage heap,
pushed asunder by the aberration of logical men.
Here in the world's rejected end
is the destined Afaningkong
the unbending Apostle of Truth
swaddled in the strong stench
of the cadavers of civilisation,
colonies of flies buzzing about him....
I do not intend to wake him from his dream... *(Pause.)*
I hear him groan already....
Listen to his testimony,
the testimony of Afaningkong
the unflinching Apostle of Truth.
I must leave the place:
he would not see me here
meditating on his plight.

(Lunatic exits pensively.)

ACT ONE

The scene is a voluminous garbage heap carrying assorted ordure.

Not far from the heap is a fire smoking lazily from beneath a tripod of rough stones. On it stands an old can which serves as a pot. A little distance away from the fire is a bundle stuffed with assortments - old tins, rags, bones, etc. Besides is a sheaf of rusty papers.

On the side of the heap, facing the fire and the bundle, CREATURE, aged about fifty, is squatted on a stone, his legs and hands brought together as if they were in chains. He has an exceptionally big long bone in his hand. He leans backward, dozing. He is almost nude except for a tattered pair of knickers that reveals part of his phallus resting on his left thigh. He remains fixed in that position staring thoughtfully into space.

As if of a sudden insight, CREATURE staggers up, bone in hand, and gathers the bundle which he thrusts under his armpit. Listens. Looks about in anticipation.

CREATURE: *(Moving staggeringly to the right side of the heap.)* That's him. That's his voice. That's his guttering voice. He comes to release me at last. For certain I will be freed... I will be released... *(Prances about in excitement.)* I will see my wife and little ones again after a long, long time. Hurray, King Traourou! *(Pauses). Looks about hopefully. No one comes in sight. No voice calls again. Resigning.)*

It cannot be Traourou. *(Listens.)* Traourou cannot come until I confess to the clan that I told a lie. Does one swear a lie by telling it? Isn't that sheer madness? *(Pauses.)* Isn't that sheer madness?

(Contemplates. Rummages heap with the aid of the bone. Selects one item of refuse and then another and stocks them in the

bundle.)

He wants me to rally the clan. Confess to them that I told a lie. *(Rummages heap.)* I cannot. Me, Afaningkong, I cannot. I tell you, I cannot.
(Returns to the place where he was first squatted. Lays the bundle to the ground and goes back to the heap. Rummages.)

I spoke the truth. How can I lie to the clan that Ganje was not dead? That he was not killed? When these eyes saw them. Saw the thugs. Saw them drag Ganje into a bush. And on towards the river. When these eyes saw the thugs masked, armed with axes and machetes. How would the clan believe me when even Womba was butchered in plain day light, in the eyes of the clan? When the clan beheld Womba's testes sliced by the butcher squad, his head cut from his trunk and taken to the Alps? And the rest of his body was chopped like a piece of bad yam. Said Womba had to face a butcher squad because he had turned terrorist, when Womba was out to save the clan like Ganje.

(Rummages heap. Finds a hard crumb of bread, retires to his seat and munches it, groans, munches. Some flies are pestering his wound. With a quick flick of the hand he catches two or three. Squeezes them in his hand, throws the content in his mouth and munches. The chewing is finished. He stares into space for an instant, picking his very dishevelled hair. Smiles, concentrates gaze, then laughs maniacally as he rises, bone in hand.)

How can I lie that they did not wrench Ganje's neck? When they turned the poor man's neck, and turned until I heard the crack of the spinal bone? Then quick, quick, they cut off Ganje's head and put in a black bag. I watched Ganje gurgling to his end. And they found a stone, tied Ganje's trunk to it and rolled it down into the river. *(Beats his chest.)* Hoi! Who can see a man's head severed from his trunk and tell the clan that it was a lie? That was Ganje gone. That was the pride of the clan gone. The hope of the clan gone. Mocked on the bottom of a river by crocodiles. His head taken to the Alps for Norman meat. Skull for Norman castles. *(Pauses. Groans and toddles about the heap. Stops.)* Can one carry a plague in the bottom of a single mind? Can one hide a plague from the clan? Can one say that the gods of the clan are not slighted? I could not carry a plague in my belly alone. I called the people and told the truth. Told the truth! And asked for a solemn funeral for Ganje. Me. I asked for a king's funeral for Ganje. The clan mourned eight days and eight nights. The gods wept eight seasons. And their tears rose from the earth. There was flood for one whole season. Until the people dug a grave. A king's grave, and buried Ganje's coffin. Ganje married to a rock in the bottom of the river. Ganje mocked in the bottom of the river by crocodiles. His head in the Alps.

(Pauses. Squats on his seat, picks the dry paste of his wound and throws in his mouth. Munches.)

The clan was furious. Was bitter with the bile of a python. Was anxious for retaliation. Then he sent throngs of liars to tell the clan that Ganje was not dead. To say that Ganje and Tum Yoye had travelled abroad to rally men against the robbers from the Alps, the robbers that stole away the good things of the clan. Used slaves like Traourou to steal away the life of the clan. To fight the caprice of imperial men. To save the people from the injustice and greed for new power, which slaves like Traourou, claimed was birthright. That Ganje was away in obscurity making new strategies. And that he wasn't dead. The clan ignored. And then it was force. Brute force. Bloody force to keep the people down. They tortured and killed and said no one must say Ganje was dead. *(Supporting his chin with his left hand.)* How can one lie to the clan and the gods? Tell the clan that I told a lie to keep them calm? *(Rises, a little agitated.)* If I spoke the truth, was it for that you dragged me into the cold underground hole? Eh! Traourou? Was it for that you grabbed me on the throat and disappeared into obscurity? Like Ganje? That you beat me, tortured me. Put pepper in my eyes. Put pepper on my thing? Tied me on the stakes and swung me out of life? Plugged current in my anus and left me hungry in the hole for years...? Wanting me to swear that I told a lie? *(Folds his arm as he shakes his head.)* Chei! Chei! Chei! I've died once. Real death. I have died beyond death. Dying slowly without a word. Without any one to pity me. What did I come to this world to do if life was death. If Traourou had killed me and thrown into a bush at once, dogs would have been happier. Worms and ants would have been happier. But I don't like dogs. Let me not see a dog here. They can not set me free. They connive easily with thieves. *(Releases fold of the arms, then with dignity.)* But I was resolute. I told them the truth how Ganje died. Spoke only the truth. Nothing but it. They took me to another hole underground. Added pepper to my thing. To my eyes. And current in my anus. But I was resolute. I told no lie that Ganje was not dead. I spoke the truth. Nothing but the truth. The other day, they dragged me to yet another hole. Very tight hole. Water on the floor. Pepper burning out my eyes and I only heard the door locked behind me. "You shall make up your mind by tomorrow!" Said the guttural throat. The water, ankle deep. You cannot lie on the floor. In water. Pepper burning out my eyes. Trickles of cold water came dripping on my head from the ceiling above. From hell above. You cannot evade it. Icy drops of cold water came dripping on my head. I could not wash my eyes, with cuffs on my legs, on my wrists. I was dying. Worse

10

death than Ganje! Oh Ganje! Ganje! I'd rather be mocked by crocodiles at the bottom of a lake than endure eternal hell in the underground. But the worst was still to come. The water on the floor changed its mind. Current. Current in it. I struggled here. Struggled there in a tight hole blind, with pepper in my eyes. So it went. I wailed. I cried. No one was anywhere. Was this the right way to die? But I was dying. I could quicken their job, stab or hang myself. But oh! The cuffs on my feet and hands!

(Heaves a sigh. Moves towards heap. Stops midway and faces front stage.)

Another morning they came. Took me out of the chamber. Death chamber. They told me things. Promised me things. The berets told me things. *(Parodying.)* "We'll send you to stay in the Alps. With your entire family. White men will do your desire. Serve you like a king. You will never know sorrow or anger or torture or poverty. We'll send you with lots of the clan's money. You will be a happy man...a king if you swear to the clan that you told a lie. If you tell them Ganje was not dead. That he was abroad on mission for the good of the entire clan. You promise to tell the clan? We go?" I said the truth. And furious, they took me to places. Did things to me I cannot remember. I cannot just remember. The old fool, Traourou himself came. Having been told I was resolved to speak nothing but the truth, he promised all. I spoke only the truth. He gave orders and the berets grabbed my throat and dragged me into a den. Torture. Hoi! Torture. I cried. I wailed and wept but they were gone, gone.

(Pauses. Looks round the heap and finds a fresh bone. He collects it and returns to his seat. Squats. Gnaws away the bits of flesh on the bone. Rises and pokes the fire which is still smoking lazily. He puts

11

down the can pot and pokes the fire again. He sets the can pot on the tripod again, picks a bone and continues to gnaw voraciously, groaning and stamping his left leg on the ground. The bits of flesh are exhausted. He throws the bone on the heap and moves round it. He rummages the rubbish with a big bone, sings and dances round the heap.)

O gina go le go	If you move alone
Mbo toh njong ééé	You'll step on thorns
Ma njah ta njaba	We mourn loud when we are many

O gina me n'nko	If you move in a group
Mbo toh mbit ééé	You will step on shit
Ma njah ta njaba	We mourn loud when we are many

O toh mbit mbit	If you step on shit
Mbe nwo sog lééé	Someone will wash your leg
Ma njah ta njaba	We mourn loud when we are many

(The song is repeated over and over as he dances round the heap, occasionally stopping to examine one item or the other on the heap. Then suddenly he stops as if of immediate thought. Walking towards his seat.)

Ganje stood for truth. Tum Yoye stood for truth. Oumi stood for truth. Womba stood for truth. They ate in truth. Breathed in truth. Slept in truth. Swore in truth. Died in truth. Their people were dying hourly. They were pining and gnashing their teeth for the pleasure of King Traourou. For the pleasure of Kingboy Traourou. Ganje wanted to see the end of it. Wanted to see the people's green lawns, their green fields and rubbish heaps swell out with fruits for the people themselves. Wanted to see their sweat swell out to the bounty of the clan and not for the thieves who

came from the Alps to drain the clan....handpicked
Traourou to auction the clan...Ganje fought to stop
these new invaders...some kind of red inglorious
beasts...came into the clan in their numbers...., each one
with one red buttock as if they sit on boiling pots....and
noses long like hooks for evil fish.... Ganje wanted to
cover the pits into which his kindred fell day and night
in Traourou's traps, their necks cut for the Alps. Their
testes sliced for king's meat. Ganje stood for truth. Was
not for the cap, which Traourou held tight to his head.
Which Traourou swore was the gift of his gods whose
winds fan the sand in the desert. Traourou's cap which
no one dared desire. Who could hazard his head by
raising his eyes to look at Traourou's cap? The road to
the hole is very smooth. Who dared raise his eyes to
look at Traourou's cap? Your head would have been
cut off for the Alps before you brought it down. You
would be pounded by berets with riffle butts, like you
would pound bad cocoyams in a rough mortar. Or you
are taken to a hole, which induced blindness. There you
lose your sight and life and only the body remains to
feel the wrath of copper whips. Even if Traourou
dreamed that someone spied his cap with desire he did
not sleep that night. And if any one crossed his eye in
the dream, and the morning came you were done with
before he went for breakfast.

*(Pauses, a wry smile on his face. He takes a few steps towards the can
pot and peeps in. He throws back his head and moves towards the
heap.)*

That's how another day he came to me, quarrelled me,
hit me on the face, spat on my face, kicked me below
the belt. Said I hid Oumi. Said he dreamed Oumi
spying his cap with desire. Said, Oumi, Womba and
Ganje wanted his cap. That Ganje had been disciplined.
And Oumi too must answer for it. That Oumi must go.

13

That Oumi's head must go to the Alps. And that I knew where Oumi was hiding. Where he was making strategies to grab his cap. Said I must show Oumi's hiding place or he blows up my head. Blows up my stubborn head and drown my family in their own blood. But I knew not where Oumi was hiding. I spoke the truth. Then came the stakes, the gnawing cold water, the current, and the pepper on my thing.... Hoi! Drown my family in their own blood! Traourou would ask that to be done before he finished breakfast. Before his spittle dried on thirsty earth. Traourou! He likes the taste of blood. The taste of fresh testes. The smell of rotting skulls. Real human skulls. Look at the Alps....A magnificent construction. Traourou's empire of the other world. Built with human skulls. Ganje's skull used for the cornerstone. When he called Oumi's name I knew he was out for his skull. For another cornerstone. I knew he was for my own skull. My family's skull. I knew I was done with. But I know not where Oumi's hiding, where he is making strategies.

Another day, not long after, two red berets come into my hole. Grabbed me on the throat and dragged me out with brutal force. Dragged me into obscurity. Very late into the night. Yes, very late into the night. Somewhere, in obscurity great Traourou was waiting. Bitter with anger. "Listen" he roared. "This be the last time I talk to a wretched goddamned brute like you. You must show where Oumi hides or you lose all, your skull and your entire family. Lead him on!" The berets led me on. They went round and round in obscurity. Great king following.... *(Pauses. Stamps his left leg on the ground.)* You can know all the roads that lead to hell but not that which leads to the underground. You can name all the holes in a termites' mound, not that road which leads to the death-hole. We went round and round. Alas, I knew where we stood. That was my house in view. That was where I must lose all. That was where my testes would be cut off to whet Traourou's appetite....

"Get on!", shouted a beret. "Show where he hides or you die". I got on to where I knew not. That was my house in view. My little ones within dreaming about a wretched father fixed in an anthill like a captured cricket. And me, on my own feet, was going to auction them for the Alps. I knew not where Oumi was hiding. And was I to lose all? "Get on!" shouted a beret. I got on. Going to Oumi's hiding that I knew not. I got on and they followed. Traourou too followed. Going to have my children's skulls yanked off for the Alps. My wife's skull cut for the Alps. I knew not Oumi's hiding. And must I lose all? I received their orders and I got on to my doom. I passed onto a graveyard. Short-cut to my slaughterhouse, to the devil's workshop. There, within a short distance my house was, my slaughterhouse, containing all that which has meaning in life for me. They followed. But I stopped in the graveyard. It was there they must bury me before they go for my little ones, my wife.... No budging from the graveyard. Here, everything about life ends. Only the cold winds of the ghosts chill the hearts. Here life is sweeter than Traourou's holes crammed with living corpses. Here ends hatred, here ends love. Here ends joy, here ends suffering. Here ends power, here ends minions. Here ends ambition, here ends despair. Here ends riches, here ends poverty. But here only one thing survives. That is Truth. The truth that all things end. "Get on!" shouted a beret. I didn't budge. They hit the riffle butt on my head. I moved a step, they followed. I stooped and knocked hard on a concrete grave calling... "Ganje! Ganje! I have brought your murderers as you required. Avenge them justly." Then I heaved a loud groan. Before I raised my head... Hi hi hi hi! They were fleeing in different directions. Hi hi hi hi! Their rifles clanging on their hips. Hi hi hi hi!

Traourou, how the old fool fled! How the devil roared and fled holding his cap firm to his head. That Traourou! Who would have thought a demigod like Traourou could fear the devil? Would be scared by a mere knock on the grave?

(Laughs fitfully. Turns and squats on his seat, bone in his hand, lays bone down, picks up the sheaf of papers, turns over a few pages. Laughs again. Drops it, takes bone, laughs even more fitfully.)

If you want to wear the black cap and red feather, you must be prepared for the wrath of ghosts. The wrath of the vengeant ghosts. If you want to wear the black cap and red feather unchallenged you must use your cuffs on ghosts. Must use your current on ghosts. Must put pepper on their things, in their eyes and drag them into holes like termites drag their captives. That is, if you want to claim the black cap and red feather you must sell your soul to the devil. Must sell it to the vengeant ghosts. Must appease them. Must not venture with one whose head lies rotting in the Alps and he walks the night without a head. Must not venture with one whose head is a cornerstone in the palace of the Alps. Must stand the wrath of ghosts whose skulls bleed in the Alps, if you want the cap and feather unavenged. Must appease the ghosts.

Or power is nothing. Only a nightmare. Only a long savage night of worry-about-nothing. Only the dry voice of a ram bleating from the rostrum in parliament, ranting of beadledom and bumbledom. Of monocracy and tribacracy, kleptocracy and meritocracy, stratocracy and imperium im imperio.... And the voice dies in the middle of a thundering applause.

Only a dry voice in crowds of sun-beaten starving countrymen, beating life out of drums hoping for hope. Crowds of sycophantic mediamen reeling off in aberration as though they were stung by evil bees,

16

hoping for hope. Power wants to smile to show concern. Ends with the smile of a corpse, teeth hanging abroad, because praise-singers may be wearing skirts of murder. Praise-singers may be blowing shafts of poisoned arrows in the melody. Praise-singers may be pulling out daggers in private to end the life of Power. The teeth of Power hangs in the sun like the teeth of an unprepared corpse.

Only dry voices pilfering here and dumping there. Stealing from the lakes and dumping in the seas, robbing from the mounds to top the mountains of the Alps. Gnawing from the hamlets and dumping in the Alps. That paradise rich in human skulls and testes. In the end the Alps plays tricks. Power loses all. The robbed lose all. The robbers lose all.

Only dry voices at lascivious luncheons. Large tables crumpling under the weight of excellent vin d'Alpine, excellent aromatized chicken and beef and bacon roasted by some devil steward in the Alps. Fermented table wine distilled from the droppings of rotting human skulls. Great ladies here. Fair teenage ladies there. Wonderful ladies sitting here and there. Fragile smiles, starry looks. Charming looks in His Excellency Power's company. Aroma. Cute aroma in the air. But His Excellency cannot dine because aroma is the cheapest device to stifle power.

Dry voices in bedchamber. How can sleep come? Next-of-kin's machete is hidden by to cut a long story short and own his father's chair. No, it isn't that. Shuffling of militiamen. Guards on duty coming for the neck? Like Ganje's neck? No, it cannot be. They are honest men. Honest tribacratic militiamen on guard in the palace. Exorbitantly paid militiamen. They cannot venture.

Or is she gone? Power turns and fumbles in the gold-wrought blanket for his sweet wife. The only consolation, the life-long spouse. So that her lustful groins can moisture sleep, digress thoughts from the worry about the enemies of Power. But whereto is she gone? To tell the vengeful ghosts that it was time to haunt so that they come for his neck? Or simply abandoned or fed up with Power's ugly mask? Instructing devil steward, the devil of a cook how to poison Power's food so that in his death she can make a solid will for herself, grab everything and flee to another man? And become the queen of all sweat, all ambitions? No, it cannot be. Or is she gone to make love to minions? Women need work, need to be worked. While you lie there browsing on the boons of power a starving sweetheart might have gone to graze on the virility of lowly men. It cannot be. But what noise? Noise from the devil's steward's bedchamber, sweetheart whimpering under the weight of devil steward rising and falling, rising, falling, grinding, crushing, pounding….

"Hoi!" maniacal voice shrieks from the armpit of a bunker. "Paradise gone to minions! Minions licking King Traourou's dish!" Hullabaloo in the palace. "Slave! Negro! Ape! Take him to the slaughterhouse! Quarter the slave. Slice his testes. Cut his throat. Congeal his blood. Do so now. Before I open my eyes let me be told that the devil steward is dead. Let me be told that the slave is dead!" And up! Up! Power hurries across the Mediterranean in search of psychiatrists in the Alps. He dies there on others' rubbish heaps. Or paraded into a hole on return by tribacratic militiamen who have changed their minds and want the cap and feather. And Power is manacled in a dungeon it built for adversaries, for the powerless...

(Observes his wrists, which have been brought together now in, cuffed position. Observes the wound on his left leg. His legs have been brought instinctively to a chained position. He wriggles both legs and wrists fitfully. Stops, wriggles more vigorously, trying in a desperate gesture to

break free from imaginary chains. Stops and contemplates. He wriggles his fists again and again screaming.)

Traourou! King Traourou! I've been here for too long. Been in the hole for too long. Come and release me from this hell-long bondage. Set me free. Send your berets to release me. Take me out of the dungeon. Free me from helotry. I know how Ganje died but know not Oumi's hiding place. Free me.

(Rises, much infuriated. He sets about beating the heap with the bone.)

Imbecile King Traourou. Kleptocratic King Traourou. Adulterous King Traourou. Bastard King Traourou. Traitor. Oppressor. Murderer of peace. Murderer of happiness. Blood sucker. Phallus eater... Free me... Free me...

(Pauses. Listens. The atmosphere is quiet. He regains his seat in contemplation. Puts bone down and picks the paste of his wound silently. A sudden smile, then he becomes much buoyant.)

How he roared and fled from ghosts! Not looking back. Ngwi, you heard him roar? Frightened, were you? Had come close to your end but I invoked the vengeance of ghosts. And they fled. They hungered for Oumi's head. And yours. And the little ones... Our dear little ones... *(Pauses. In attentive mood.)* My dear woman, that was their want if I did not show them Oumi's hiding. But I spared your life and that of the little ones by miracle. By the miracle of ghosts. *(Pauses and becomes more attentive.)* You ask if he comes looking for me? Yes Ngwi, if he comes we're done with. They will drag me on stones for miles and have my head churned before they get it to the Alps. And you and the little ones, they'll make splinters of you. *(Pauses. Unruffled attention.)* What do you say woman? *(Pauses as before.)* We must move from here?

19

Move from this house? No. It is not possible. They can't come. They dread the graveyard and its tenants. If you only heard how the devil himself roared and fled. All the gunpowder in the palace could not make him brave. Gunpowder is for men who have flesh. *(Pauses. A little snobbishly.)* That's woman's talk, Ngwi, Madwoman's talk. Your head isn't good. No woman kept her head for good sense. Unfortunate things! God spent too much time on their beauty that time cut him short. The seventh day cut him short. Lucifer cut him short and they were left hollow and frail. *(Pauses.)* You're only a woman, Ngwi. That's how you insist. But I say they won't come! *(Pauses as before.)* You are talking foolish talk Ngwi, mad woman's talk. The clan is behind me. We'd survive in their midst and protection. How can you say the clan is not loyal in supporting my cause? How can you think the clan is capricious? They have shown every evidence of their loyalty to my cause. *(Pauses.)* I say the people can't change their minds even for a million crowns. They are behind me. I tell them the truth. *(Pauses.)* I had to wait for time to come. I mean the clan. And they would wield their machetes, their pikes, their spears. The clan would frown and the tears of the gods would drop. Stop talking nonsensical talk Ngwi. You are only a woman. I tell you the truth. *(Pauses, then a little agitated.)* I see you weep, Ngwi. Please, don't! Don't! We'll be protected. We'll be released. We'll be freed. We'll be safe after all. *(Pauses. Hesitatingly.)* No. Not hate you. Not the children. All is for your protection, my dear woman. I don't hate you, don't hate anyone. *(More relaxed and soothing.)* Remember Ngwi, I have never seen any woman born of a woman so enchanting as you are. So ravishing, yet so understanding, so devoted. You are a gift from my god. The leopard's skin, the elephant's tusk. In short, the antiquity of the clan so endeared to me. Without you Ngwi, what is life to me, what is death to me? I fight

20

for honour, so that you can be honoured. If I succeed you'd be the most honoured of ladies in the clan. You'd be the envy of all women. Your name will be sung in history books and students shall read them for times and times without end. I get trapped in the hole for your honour. To convince you that I am a man. You Ngwi, are really wonderful. Imagine the last days before they were up for Oumi's head, for your head and that of the little ones. Imagine me in that cold death house without you. That cold cave without you, Ngwi. All alone. And you come into mind... Hi! hi! hi!... I was moved. I was elated like a charged particle in a magnetic field. I was hot, hot, hot to splitting. Hi! hi! hi! I felt the warmth of your breath in my eyes, my ears, and on my entire face. Everywhere. I felt the pulsing of your breasts beating in my heart, the palpitation of your groins...quem...quem...quem. Ah, the lustful thighs you used to wrap me in and induce me to sleep and conjure my heaven. And we roll here and there in that sugary paradise. And you pull my hair, crying softly, "No! no! no!" yet urging me on. Hi! hi! hi! I was hot in the hole to splitting. Really hot till the pepper abandoned my thing and the pains of manacles deserted my wrists. *(Pauses)* Ah! Those delicacies you used to cook for me. My abeh nchi! My achu and black soup! My corn fufu and njama njama, my ekwankolo, my atimanambussa! Khahti-khahti! *(Pauses)* Ngwi, do you know you are an unmatched mistress in kitchencraft? I thought about you the other day when the berets....those mad boys drugged by Traourou came into my hole. They had starved me for six days...for six good days. And I was weary. Really weary to death. It was only hunger that kept me alive. And you know that hunger is like a plague. It visits you like a joke and when there is nothing to appease it, it breaks you down and consumes you.... Traourou's men came on the seventh day and told me that His Unrivalled Highness, Majesty

King Traourou, The Giver and Taker of Life has offered me a meal on his ninety-ninth birthday. They brought out a package wrapped in wax paper. It looked like cake. And they brought out a bottle of mimbo that looked like *vin de messe*. My eyes brightened. King Traourou! His Majesty King Traourou! The Giver and Taker of life! He might change his mind at last, release me. *(Kneeling, his eyes closed and hands brought together on his chest as in prayer)* I believe in one God, His Imperial Majesty King Traourou the First Unlimited, Emperor of Infinite Dominions, The Giver and Taker of Life, King beyond King, Life beyond Life, Life after Life, I believe in you.... Thank you, my god for not taking my life yesterday. Thank you, almighty, for giving me life today...Thank you....thank you....thank you....thank you....thank you your Majesty for giving me life today. May you live for nine hundred and ninety-nine years renewable! Amen. Amen. Amen. *(Rises and as he moves away hastily with a repulsive indignation)* Mmff! Mmff! It smelt of old shit when I loosened it. King Traourou's shit that had been left to bake in the sun for days. The mimbo, mmff! mmff! It was the smell of a mad man's urine. A mad man called Traourou whose piss was left for days to ferment. Mmff! Mmff! I pushed it aside. *(Tying his lips firmly against his nose and still saying "Mmff! Mmff!")*. They grabbed my testes, squeezed them and said I must eat. Weighed my testes in their palm and said, healthy meat for His Majesty's dinner, then squeezed hard my testes again like you would squeeze the chaff of an orange and said I dared not refuse His Majesty's charity on his birthday. Chained my hands again, quick, quick and forced the shit into my mouth. Washed it into my belly with the piss. You must eat the King's entrails on his birthday, they said. The elements within me revolted. But the muscles of my belly were too weak to resist....Too weak to vomit out the madness of King Traourou. They hit my head and mouth with the butts of rifles till my jaws were spongy with bleeding. They blocked the door of the hole and my next visitor was the rising water on the floor, electric current in it....*(Pauses, then indignantly.)* Woman, you've lost your head, unh? *(Pauses.)* There is water rumbling in it, unh? I hunger for you that's why we must stay here and go nowhere. *(Pauses, then consoling.)* Don't Ngwi, don't go. Don't leave me in the cold. You must never leave me alone...you are the only friend I have in this whole damned world.... *(Pauses. With agitation.)* No. *(As before.)* Headstrong woman! I say no. *(Pauses.)* The little ones. *(Pauses.)* A charming mother. *(Pauses.)* Demons. *(Pauses.)* Phantoms. *(Pauses.)* Swines guffawing. Crickets snorting. Crabs yawning. Neophytes pounding stones.

(Rises and sets about scattering waste on the garbage heap hysterically. He returns to the fire to poke it. Turns to the heap and continues rummaging.)

Owls gargling. Stragglers crooning... *(Stops abruptly. Looks exasperated.)* I smell the blood of my little ones. I smell the blood of Ngwi. I smell it. I smell it. Traourou has been at work lynching them, lynching my little ones to keep the cap. I smell their blood.

(Carries his hands on his head in a lament as in a funeral as he weeps round the heap.)

Hoi! Hoi! Kingboy, Your will is done. Hoi! King Traourou, your will is done. Manor of rotting skulls and testes, your will is done. Hoi! Lion of the Alps, your will is done.... Giver and Taker of life, your will is done. You have murdered all the chicken in the clan to wear the feathers. *(Hitting his lips with his palm.)* Wu-tu-u-u-u-u-u! Traourou! You have peeled off the feathers on our backs to dress your cap. Wu-tu-u-u-u-u! What am I left with? Of what use am I? Why was I even born? What reason did he give? Who said I should live, live in a hole like a rat? But even a rat can be eaten by Traourou. Why can't Traourou devour me like a lion and serve his appetite? Of what use am I in the hole? Hoi, Traourou! You have done a thing to me that tongues never can tell.

(Sits on a stone, then lies on the heap on his back. His hands are still clasped on his head as he mourns in a low tone, which gradually drops as he doses off.)

ACT DROPS

Lunatic strides stealthily to a near corner of the stage.

Lunatic:
> The prophet has gone to sleep....
> What fractured imaginings does he
> compose in his dreams
> under this searing tropical sun,
> in this hot, acrid air?
> These men are divine
> who are cast away by the vanity
> of civilised men
> to seek life in death on refuse heaps
> because their tongues are barbarous
> and their ways are wild
> like the wild birds of the sky.
>
> They are not wise, they are not rich,
> salacred on junks of sane waste
> cursed by men that trade on reason
> to gnaw their dung and drink their filth
> and live like the beggarly children of the universe.
> Here is Afaningkong repressed, flies
> nibbling his carcass
> like wolves would tear the body
> of a dying sheep.
>
> Yet we are all men
> who on our first day
> walked naked on the shores of life
> making dirt our friend
> and prancing about it in delirium,
> we are all men
> flawed with insanity
> of passion and ambition;
> we are all men
> toiling after death's dark desire;
> we are all men

clung to the faltering claim
of wisdom, logic and reason,
Yet, we are all mad men
chasing civilisation
like children
tracking their own shadows.

But where is their fate:
these undying generations on the heap
squawking and dancing
with smiles
far away from life
of thinking men?

Wrapped in unfettered worlds
they climb the imagination
rung by rung
till they reach God's home.
They are diviners,
pass them quietly
because you wake them from the dream....
(Pause. Creature groans audibly) I hear the Apostle stir.
Afaningkong, the Apostle of Truth, he stirs.
I must go away lest I wake him
from his dream.

(Exit Lunatic.)

ACT TWO

Scene is the same. It is afternoon. A little ray of smoke is seen trailing out from the fireplace. More flies are plaguing the heap and Creature's wound. Creature, still lying on his back opens his eyes and looks about wearily. He struggles and sits up looking agitated. He collects bone, yawns and scratches his belly with the bone, yawns and turns towards the refuse heap. He staggers to his feet and yawns again, this time more elaborately, scratches his neck and starts turning over refuse on the heap with bone.

Creature: *(In anticipation.)* I thought I heard someone speak. I thought a beret came by to remove me from this hole. Or, at least to throw food on the heap for me. *(Disappointed.)* They have not come round for long. There are no fresh bones on the heap. No bread crumbs. *(Turns over garbage with bone.)* Only old tins. Plastics. Paper. Dirt. *(Searches more thoroughly.)* They don't come to throw food for me any more. *(Searches.)* Everything is dry. Dry. Dry. Dry bones. Dry sticks, dry tins, dry rags. The bones, you can hardly have a pinch from the bones. Nothing. *(Searches.)* Hope he comes. I'm weary of the hole. Been too long in the hole. *(Searches.)* Hope when it shall rain Traourou will let the termites out of their holes, me with them. Hope he'll send the berets to open the gates of the termites' holes and send me to freedom. It isn't a good place. Only a dry place, cold place, a death place.

(Searches. Concentrates gaze on an item of refuse. He picks it, holds it to his nose, shakes his head and throws the item back to the heap.)

The hole isn't good. The berets don't come to throw food to me in the grave any more. Even if they have been asked to show where Oumi hides, let them come straight to me. And I will tell them that I know not where Oumi's hiding. I will tell them that the hole isn't

27

a good place for me. I will tell them the truth how Ganje died. So that they send me out into the world. Ganje is gone. He isn't stifled in the hole like me.

(Searches. Finds nothing to eat. He returns to the fire discouraged and starts poking it, peeps into the pot and does not find any thing to eat. He sits on a stone with his hands clasped on his head in contemplation then picks the dry paste of his wound and throws in his mouth. Munches.)

Does he live? I don't hear him roar any more. That lion of the jungle of the Alps. He doesn't come threatening and thundering here any more. I don't see the berets any more... *(Pauses. Contemplates.)* Two of his henchmen passed here. My two countrymen he lured to the other side of the Great River with throngs of men to betray and cut their heads. And they killed Bobe Khom. Their ghosts passed back home snivelling in the night. They stopped by and pined for a little warmth of my fire. I said nothing. They squawked and begged and I said nothing.

"All's not well," they said. "All's not well. Running on the wheels of power to wear cap and feather, we caught a cold in Shwaart, in Mbrouhngwi. We lost everything. We are on our way home." I was frightened.

"Where is Traourou?" I said.

"He went abroad," they said. "His ghost is hovering around the palace and his kid brother is so frightened".

"The berets!" I asked.

"They have run amuck," they said. "They want the cap where Traourou's head is entrenched. Could we come for the fire?"

"And the throngs of men you led to the other side of the river?" I asked.

"We sold them with their heads and testes and their blood. But they weren't enough. We could sell the whole land but that would not be enough to wear the cap for a day."

"Why didn't you wait a little longer, and hope and cut heads and hope?" I asked.

"It was no use", said the one who had dried and puckered up like the stem of a dead yam, his large eyes rolling in his skull like two minor spheres. "It was no use being fixed in a shop window. They didn't even give me food after I had done all, sold my people and changed the course of the Great River."

The other said, "They said I had grown older than Methuselah and I was shamelessly greedy for Her Majesty's crumbs. That I was too old to wash her Majesty the Painted Queen's linens. They assigned me to wash the latrine and kill cockroaches. If I complained, they hit my bald head. An old man's bald head. I grew weaker and weaker with age and the swinging of the broom till I could hardly breathe any more. Could we come for the fire?" they asked.

(Creature pauses. Rises bone in hand, as if of sudden consternation. He moves furiously and hurriedly towards the right of the heap.)

Let me ask you. Where is Bobe Khom? Why did you kill him? Why did you kill life? Why did you kill history? Why did you kill posterity? Why…, why did you kill the man who would have set down the load of troubles on your head now? Why did you kill him? You wanted posts from Traourou. You wanted to lick Traourou's buttocks! *(Clasps his hands and moans)* And they killed the prophet. And they killed Bobe Khom on our own side of the Great River. Go away tempters. Go away and don't tempt me any more. You desired that I live in a hole till I rot, you and your man, Traourou. I don't understand why you come here in ugly shapes to tempt me. I know how Ganje died but not Oumi's hiding. Release me if you want. Or you go away from my sight. You showed greed for the cap and feather, and you must leave me alone if you'll not release me. Swindlers, sell-outs, butchers, traitors! Send your berets and I'd leave the hole for you.

(Returns to the seat. He does not squat yet. He turns instead towards the direction from which he came - the right side of the heap. He sighs and shakes his head.)

They'd not come here into the hole to ask for charity. I swear I'd drive them all away. I'd chase them out with this sceptre. *(Brandishes bone.)* I'd quarter them all with this hand. I'd quarter them all. Those traitors of hope. I'd quarter them all. *(Flexes out his chest to assume a posture of majesty, then pointing to the heap.)* I am manor of this lot. Not by conspiracy or intimidation. Who contests with me here? Let him show up if he won't lose his head. *(Takes dignifying steps round the heap.)* It's my natural right and belonging. *(Points to the stone.)* This is my throne. *(Moves towards the stone and squats on it with dignified airs. Brandishes bone.)* And this is my sceptre. They call me Afaningkong the Great because I have all of these on the heap, by natural right. For all these, clans have extinguished clans and brothers have murdered brothers. For all these, all kinds of insanity have taken control of the world. The one who says he can no longer cope with poverty and chooses the noose. He thinks his god is unkind if he cannot give him a few of these dry crumbs to make him rich. The other one who casts lots in witch houses staking his little ones, one by one to raise a fortune and become as great as I am. Another one, squatted in some bar, her buttocks raised in the air like those of a soldier ant. She would tell every one that she is making tough lady. Is that not madness? That vendor of her parts. She wants to raise money to acquire a bit of my junk, what she calls making herself beautiful. There is the shitman scratching the last grain off his fellow's bottoms. There is the toppler of clans, thugs wrenching necks. All slaves of creation, here is their desire. *(Pointing to the garbage heap.)* From here all beauty grows and all ugliness flourishes. And people crushing other's heads call it their own. This is what Traourou wants. But he first must drain every blood in pipelines to his mentors' storehouses in the Alps. To his empire of the other world. An empire of fine construction with Ganje's heads. He must ensure there is gnashing of teeth, the clan in desolation. He must have it all alone. That slave called Traourou. They say his mother migrated from a northern desert country as a prostitute. And from an accident in her professional life a great man was born. A traitor was born. The king of thugs was born. He became vengeful for knowing no father, no relative. And sought through foul means to emerge a great man when the gods of the clan were asleep. And became king of thugs. Three decades, wailing was the laughter of infants and the silent groaning of afflicted mothers. Three decades were decades of fear and terror, with the smashing of fathers' heads and wailing for heads that were lost. Trunks of men littered the streams and the earth. But Traourou was at work, wrenching necks, smashing heads and draining blood...

(Pauses. Sings and dances round the heap in a kind of mournful gait, using the bone as a dancing-machete.)

Ndogo akaba keebi o luiu befin é é	If your brother harvests plums You'll eat black ones
Ndogo afeih keebi	If your brother falls from a plum tree
o leh a'achia	you'll have sleepless nights
Ye-e- eh ye-e- eh beguo ekab keebi qwuik	*Ye-e- eh ye-e- eh* Strangers have harvested our

31

	plums
buik feh tuu	and we have fallen from the
	plum tree
Ye-e- eh ye-e- eh	*Ye-e- eh ye-e- eh*

(Stops singing and dancing. Seeming tiredness. He goes to the fire and pokes. Returns to his seat, puts bone near the bundle and clasps his hands on his head. Pause. Rises, collects the sheaf of papers, flips through the pages then holds a certain page in front of him.)

Creature: Here is the declaration. We, the indigenous people of this clan on this day of Our Lord, hereby profess our lives to total commitment to the liberation of our people from all forms of oppression, exploitation…. *(There is some weird noise that is sustained for sometime. Creature starts and listens. The noise is heard again and a voice speaks.)*

Voice: Find me a crumb of bread.

Creature: *(Looks about in confusion and staggers up from seat. About to flee.)* Who speaks? I hear a voice but see not the mouth that speaks.

Voice: Find me just a crumb of bread. I'm starving.

Creature: *(In consternation.)* May I know who you are? Would you come out plain? Stand where I can see you.

Voice: You cannot see me.

Creature: *(Anxiously.)* How that?

Voice: Day does not shine on me.

Creature: *(More anxious.)* How…how then do I give you what you want?

Voice: Put it where you stand and I shall have it.

Creature: *(Petrified.)* But… who are you?

Voice: A spirit. Traourou's spirit.

Creature: Hoi! *(He scrambles straight for bone and bundle and escaping from the heap.)* Hoi! Traourou's ghost!

Voice: Please, I'm pleading. Don't run away. Save me from starvation. Just a crumb of bread.

Creature:	*(Stops a few paces from the heap, panics.)* How comes this? Where is your body?
Voice:	Buried abroad. It ended there.
Creature:	In the Alps?
Voice:	No. Elsewhere.
Creature:	*(Very disturbed.)* Why not in the Alps?
Voice:	The Alps befouled me and I lost all. Everything that I stood for. Everything that I fought for. All's lost. I met psychiatrists and they told me I was dying. They punctured my heart with a pin and let life seep out of me gradually to my end. Saying all would be well for me. So I could continue my vocation...
Creature:	Wrenching necks?
Voice:	That's it. But shortly after that I was hurled out of the Alps to die gradually elsewhere. I wept for the remaining days of my life for all that was lost. Oh, my cap and feather!
Creature:	And your skulls and testes and tanks of blood.
Voice:	Everything. They deceived me and I took away everything from the clan to their country. When I was desperate they rejected me. They would not even allow me to live on their refuse dumps. Those people are not good friends. All that's left is my spirit. I walk the nights and days hungrily. I haven't tasted any good thing for a long time. Everything disavows me. I haunted the night for food. The night became so chilly. I waited for the clan to make a solemn funeral for me. I craved them to carry my remains back home but nothing happened. The night became so chilly for a stranger ghost and I returned to the clan.
Creature:	*(A little embarrassed.)* Could any man born of the magic of the penis grab the cap from your head, Traourou?
Voice:	No man could. No cunning, no force could. It

was all my fault, my greed for more power. Oh, Traourou, Traourou! What is this thing called power? What do men really call power? Is it a keen-edged sword with a greasy handle? Is it the melting fat of the tyrant when the anger of the clan is aflame? Who could have believed that me, Traourou, who had the hammer and the nail, who sued unsued, who gave life and took it away at will, could lose the grip of power as at child's play? Those times when Traourou merely coughed fears and fevers ran through the nerves of the clan. But all has come to naught. All naught. I yearned to be something more than a trifle of a king. Wanted to be something like a king-god. I confided in a boy in the process. But, oh treachery, treachery! A boy I had trained for years to be a weakling. A fool who is not born of the bellows and the forge of this country's loins. His father was a rogue in a southern forest country, who fled from his prosecutors into the clan. He benefited from some confusion of an unfortunate woman and a great rogue was born. A sly thief, a foolish burglar was born. A lunatic boy who bleats like sick sheep. Oh, my cap and feather! He took king's cap, wore it on his head and resisted my claim of it with idiotic stubbornness...

Creature: *(With sarcastic sympathy.)* A feast of bastards in the palace! And your berets, they didn't intervene? I mean when the sick sheep wore king's cap, wore the crown of bastards. They didn't use their rifles and their cuffs?

Voice: They're all whores, just like those blood suckers in the Alps. They changed their minds immediately with my cap and left me bald. My barber took off the last tuft of hair from my head. That was the last thing my body felt. That was the end of it as though the hair was the last string of life. I vamoosed from my body before any funeral rite could impound my ghost. Since then I have remained in the cold, sauntering here and sauntering there. Walking the night isn't comfortable and the day is too dry. It's hunger that drives me out of the shade to look for food in the day.

Creature: What will you do now?

Voice: I'm worried, very worried. I don't know where to go to or what to do. Sometimes I hang on people's doors in the evenings and listen to their gossips. Sometimes I mix up in assemblies in the palace courtyard. Or spend all days on beaches. But what is the sense in all that? I have become bored and restless. But what can I do?

Creature: *(Thoughtfully.)* Why don't you go to hell?

Voice: Hell has rejected me.

Creature: And heaven?

Voice: I have no friend in heaven.

Creature: The Alps?

Voice: There is more evil in the Alps than I ever knew or did. A ghost can be tried and strangled in the Alps.

Creature: Why not hang on a leaf like air and rock it?

Voice: I shall do that when in the end there is no answer....

Creature: The end of bastardom?

Voice: *(Ignoring.)* If in the end my corpse is not brought home and my spirit is allowed in the cold for long I shall shake the foundations of the earth. My wrath shall be felt in the fury of the tempest. There shall be mourning more than has ever been heard, if in the end I don't have a resting place. The clan must give me at least some honour for all the inhumanity I showed

	them. There is always something good in every devil. The clan should at least consider that I did some good. Give me a crumb, I'm starving.
Creature:	*(Sighs, puts down the bone and bundle and squats on the stone in contemplation.)* Then I'd never be freed.
Voice:	You talk of freedom! The worst is still to come. Many in the clan are choking than you can understand. There is ravenous misery, acute famine. The barns are dry. The wells are dry. Life in the clan is dry. The day stands weird with starvation. Now tell me, which is kinder evil? Cutting men's necks at once or starving them to death? That is the day. A grim day. When Traourou wrenched necks there was sighing. Now is weeping. My bastard brother has run mad, suffering from chronic indecision. The palace is filled with robbers, butchers, lepers, maniacs, traitors...who have taken advantage of his idiocy to wreck the clan. The idiot calls himself a democrat in order to defend his foolishness, a seed too large for him to swallow. I never could try it, even with all my wisdom. What does power gain in being democratic?
Creature:	Being the tyrant that you are, how could you try it?
Voice:	There it is, my man. There are only two kinds of governance. A ruler should choose to be either a tyrant or a democrat. A tyrant rules with the barrel of the gun, and that was me. A democrat must be an intelligent man, a very intelligent man. One who is capable of weaving events expertly to convince and outwit an always critical community. One thing in both systems is evident - there must be a line of action. But my lunatic brother ran into democracy with over-zealousness, without

objectives. And because of his incompetence, all tribes of rogues who work with him in the palace have seized the opportunity to ruin the clan and enrich themselves, threatening to murder him in bits if he attempted to resign. Now there is no order and the clan has become lifeless. You can only hear the breathing of choking men, of gagging children, of strangulating mothers. There is a terrible plague in the clan. My bastard brother has auctioned the clan for fine red Alpine wine. That's why he croaks like an overfed toad. He has battered the hearts of people for the smiles of the Lords in the Alps. He thinks that he's amongst the Alps best favoured maniacs. But he shall end up much worse than me. The clan is in trouble. You are better here.

Creature: But I told the truth. I told how Ganje died and knew not Oumi's hiding. Can I now be freed?

Voice: You refused to reveal the secret of your group.

Creature: I could not betray the clan for your selfish ends.

Voice: That's the point. You never did the volition of a tyrant. How could you then be freed? You chose to stand for truth and fought for the common man's right. I know these were good ideas at the time, which won for us the confidence of the clan and the victory to power...

Creature: And you turned tyrant, turned thug, disregarded the reasons for which we fought for change, raised your berets and barrels to oppress and maim the people, stifle the clan. When I redressed you, you turned against me, ground me in the mills of your prisons and finally blocked me in the underground hole forever...Can I now be freed?

Voice: There my young man is where you fumbled.

Who ever ruled the clan by the word of truth? You must be crafty in setting the pace of the clan. I mean you must be political if you want to rule. Truth has many roads and used by different people. Even then, which tyrant ever dined on the same table with learned men like you? Learned men are a nuisance to the man of power. They are very treacherous to the noble claims of tyranny. I dreaded you in particular. You could in a twinkle of an eye sway the clan against my omnipotence. Especially as your new alliance was with my greatest enemies whose heads I wanted with greatest urgency. You betrayed me still. I later found Oumi's hiding. He had fled from the clan and settled abroad, in a country on the other side of the Alps. I sent two boys on mission with instructions to spice his meal and bring back his skull and testes. They did my will. That was his end and I felt safe.

Creature: You have no conscience, Traourou. You have no conscience. I tried to appeal to your conscience...to make you feel the plight of the people...the sufferings of the people...to make you understand that the lords of the Alps are only out to use you to ruin the clan....

Voice: Who told you a man of power has a conscience? The vaulting claim to power can never be softened by the voice of conscience. No way. Conscience in the man of power is dead, dead. He has no emotions, no sentiments, no feelings or anything or whatever you book people will call it. It is the plight of the people, the gnashing of their teeth that gives the man of power delight, that makes him feel some pride and weight. If a man of power allowed himself to be ridden by sentiments or any related evil,

	then he is a finished man, a condemned man. Only a eunuch whose testes sizzle in the frying pan in the Alps can swear on the feet of the iron god and allow conscience to govern him.
Creature:	*(Pacing about.)* I see what you mean. The man of power strides from one evil to the other, grinding testes in his jaws, smashing testes with the butts of riffles, cutting necks and drinking blood from shattered skulls, burying men alive, heads first, purging shit in the mouths of innocent men. In the end power is nothing but a long night of hope and dream and fear and horror and fright....
Voice:	But Traourou, oh gods and devils! Me, I had good sport, good entertainment fit for a tyrant. I was an unmatched master in the art of tyranny. But my cap and feather! How it was lost! How easily power abandoned a happy king! Those cunning fellows in the Alps! They took away my life when it was sweetest. When I was at the helm of power. Ah, those sniffing devils in the Alps! They showed me paradise and took it away again. Ah me. Give me a crumb of bread, I'm starving.
Creature:	That's it. Only power can destroy power. Power, like evil, feeds on its own testes in the end. It does not reign forever. The higher the realms of vaulting ambitions for power, the shorter and fatal the time of its own destruction.
Voice:	You speak truth, my man. Oh, how could Traourou have known? Please, give me a crumb of bread.
Creature:	*(Tottering about and brandishing bone agitatedly.)* There is no crumb for you, man of power. Go to the Alps where power is stowed in the custody of imperialmen and leave me alone.

There is no conscience on the refuse dump for men of power. Go to the Alps where conscience is dead, where people survive without conscience. There, you may find salvation. *(His voice rises with indignation.)* Where are the heads you cut Traourou? Where are the true born heroes of the clan, Traourou? Oh, gods of my ancestors! *(Quick stagger to front stage.)* Where is Ganje? Where are Oumi, Yoye, Womba? Where is Bobe Khom? Where did you stow away the hope of the clan? Why did you block me in the hole forever when I spoke the truth to save the clan? To save the clan from the machinations of bastards? When do you send your berets to release me. Tell me, Traourou.

Voice:	How could you be released when you threatened a tyrant?
Creature:	*(Softly.)* Then I'd remain in the hole forever.
Voice:	I'm in the cold forever. No flesh to clothe my spirit.
Creature:	I'm damned.
Voice:	I'm starved. Give me a crumb.
Creature:	*(Perplexed, he looks about disappointedly, then sternly.)* When do you say I'd be liberated, freed? I mean, when do you send your boys, your berets to release me?
Voice:	They did that a long time ago. Give me a crumb.
Creature:	What's the meaning of that?
Voice:	*(Softly.)* You'd been released.
Creature:	*(More perplexed.)* How then am I?
Voice:	You ignored my orders, ignored the pain my boys inflicted on you, defied the stings of the electric current, winked at thrashing and the cuffs and the chains, insisted on your stand. I was prepared to keep you blocked in the

	underground prison until you confessed your crime against tyranny. You were resolute and talked only of truth.
Creature:	*(Pertinently.)* How then do you say that I was released?
Voice:	I couldn't keep you any longer. It wasn't any use. You merely occupied the places of fruitful victims who waited to take their turns. So we cast you away.
Creature:	*(Thoughtfully.)* Does my wife, I mean Ngwi, know about all this? Does she know that I'd been released?
Voice:	*(Weird laughter.)* Her skull is thriving in the Alps. Soon as I got you after your escape at the graveyard she too was done with.
Creature:	And my little ones?
Voice:	They too were done with.
Creature:	*(Loud scream)* Wutu-u-u-u! What have you done Traourou? What is my use in this world now that you killed those little ones. Wutu-u-u-u! Come and hear my own stories. Is it a dream? Even those little ones? Wutu-u-u-u!
Voice:	Their skulls weren't strong enough for cornerstones, you know. But they were used to block rat holes in the palace. I couldn't spare them. That was my policy. If you got the viper you must of necessity crush its young ones, crush the eggs too. Without which all your effort is vain, wasted labour.
Creature:	Wu-tu-u-u-u! How many times have you killed me, Traourou? *(Half-singing and half-dancing in a mournful gait.)* Who will go tell Ganje there is the acrimony of bastards in the palace of the clan? Who will go tell Womba, tell Oumi, tell Yoye, Bobe Khom that the gods of the land have been slighted? Who will calm the fury in the veins of the gods of the clan, now that

Ganje and his men are dead and gone, their trunks chopped by crocodiles in the bottom of the river? Who would cleanse the clan that is pregnant with a plague, now that the harbingers of truth are dead and gone, their skulls fixed in the palace of the Alps? The womb of the clan is heavy with misery and death. Who will appease the anger of the gods? Quell the fury of the ancestors, their bones creaking in their graves, now that Ganje is dead and gone? *(With fury)* Traourou, release me. I have been in the hole for too long. Let me go and see my children.

Voice: I say you have been released.

Creature: *(Looking worried.)* How then do you say that I have been released when I was resolute?

Voice: You weren't any good. You no longer knew right and wrong. You couldn't make a difference between life and death, night and day. You had lost your head.

Creature: To the Alps?

Voice: No. It wasn't necessary. You had lost it.

Creature: *(Twisting his neck and shaking his head.)* But I carry it with me. I speak through it. *(Holds his head and shakes it from side to side.)* I have my head with me. *(Feels his mouth.)* And a mouth too. Let me see if my mouth speaks. *(Emphatically.)* Afaningkong's mouth, speak! Speak, let me hear! *(Prances about in excitement.)* Ho-ho-ho! My mouth speaks. I'm alive. Ho-ho-ho! Traourou never cut my head for the Alps. I never lost my head. Traourou never could have it. Ho-ho-ho! How do you say I lost my head?

Voice: I say you lost it. It was of no use to the Alps. It was already demented, fragmented. It could not serve the Alps, so we threw you out into the street.

Creature:	*(Very worried, he shakes his head from side to side again and heaves a sigh.)* So I cannot be freed?
Voice:	I say you have been liberated, released. You are better still than any man living. You do not count the days and nights. You do not bother about how to feed the little ones. You care not about looking responsible, about general needs, which are the preoccupation of a sane humanity. You do not hang on the palace gates whining and envying all that was lost. You have enough on the heap. Please give me a crumb of bread. I'm starving.
Creature:	*(Sternly.)* Send your berets.
Voice:	I say you no longer need them. You lost your head in the underground prison and you were thrown out, released. Give me the bread.
Creature:	*(Collecting bone and rising with furious indignation.)* What's this madness? Go away you starving wizard. Go, devil. I have nothing for you. Go haunt and beg in the Alps where you have made fortunes out of wretched men.
Voice:	Please, only a crumb.
Creature:	*(Hysterically.)* I say leave me alone, wizard. No crumbs for tyrants.
Voice:	Then I am damned.
Creature:	And starved. Go straight to the Alps.
Voice:	Please, only a crumb.
Creature:	I say leave me alone, you bastard. Go to the country of the devil and beg. Send your berets to release me. Send them to free me. I have been underground for too long. I want to be freed so that I can see my children. And you come instead, asking for crumbs. Go straight to the Alps. There's good store there for four decades that you have been the unrivalled king. Go, demon, and be damned in the Alps.

(Pause. Voice is not heard again. Creature stares round suspiciously, then blinking as he weeps.)

Gods of my ancestors, bastards have brought woe to the clan. Tyrants have wreaked havoc on the clan. A red feather on a king's black cap is no more the committed token of love and service to the clan. Traourou and his imperialmen have brought in a throng of bastards and stolen kingship, stolen the rights of the people, stolen the happiness of the people. How can the clan survive with a king whose ancestry can not be traced? Who then would offer sacrifices if the gods are angry? Whose ancestors are to be evoked to commune with the gods? Oh, Traourou, what a black day for the clan? *(More unnerved.)* You would not cut necks because you feel the nerve of your own blood. You would not feed on testes because you taste the taste of your own balls. You would not cut necks because you feel the nerve of your own flesh, because you have a conscience, a lineage belonging. How could Traourou have a nerve for the clan, enh? How could he? He has no sympathies. He has no feeling for the blood that is spilt on the earth of the clan. How can he have when he has no relations to feel for? How can the beast feel?

It is a cataclysm of misery. Bastards have desecrated the shrines of the clan. One bastard succeeding the other. And the gods and ancestors must be appeased. Some clansman who can count his ancestors from the beginning of time must lead the procession to the ancestral shrine. Some clansman whose black cap and red feather is linked with the umbilical cord of the gods and ancestors of the clan. He must lead the clan to a sacrifice of pacification and expiation. Death is on the clan's shores. Someone must lead the clan to a sacrifice. A thousand bastards, thousand sheep, thousand swines, thousand cattle must

44

be slaughtered and the blood sprinkled in the nave of Fuandem's shrine. So that the god's fury can subside. So that our ancestors can put down their heads, continue their rest and save the tribulation. The gods must be appeased. *(Sternly.)* And there must be an end to bastardom and the beginning of Truth if the clan shall be saved. And that truth lies in the graves of the ancestors and in the shrines of the gods. How could Traourou build an empire on murder and suppression? Enh, how could he? Traourou's ghost must be impounded. Must be....

(Beats about the heap. A weird sound is heard again, this time a little louder. Creature's mouth is wide open. He begins to shiver, tries to sit but falls on his buttocks on the heap. The shivering intensifies as he cries out.)

Hoii!... Where are these from...hoii...apparitions... ghosts with fractured skeletons....rumblings...the world is cleaving...hills pounding valleys...ghosts mad in a weird rite chortle in obsequies...thousand heads singing anthems roll down the Alps...rumblings...seas sneaking into new valleys...palace walls crumbling, ghettos crumbling. A huge flood... The flood.... *(His voice grows very loud.)* Stop flood! Stop f-l-o-o-d! *(Still shivering as he staggers to his feet.)* Hoi! Traourou's ghost is hanging on a leaf and the end is near!

(Weird noise is heard again, very loud. Bewildered, he flees a few paces from the heap. He looks at the bone, the sheaf of papers and the bundle lying near the stone, moves stealthily towards the heap, collects them and flees back again.)

Hoi! Hoi! You see? Hoi! Has the day come to this? What madness? What ill luck have bastards brought to the clan?

(Takes short cautious strides to the other side of the heap but without getting close to it.)

Hoi! Traourou! Was it a plan of yours to untie the knots of the earth and let it crumble on my head? What mad world! Mad Traourou! Mad, mad King Traourou! Send your berets....So I can be freed... *(Loud)* Traourou....Traourou....Free me....Fre-e-e-e me-e-e....

(Stands shivering, his eyes wide open, his mouth agape as he breathes heavily. The bone is in his hand and the bundle in his armpit. Swoons.)

(Enter Lunatic with a saddened countenance and a deadened tempo.)

Lunatic:
       I know
       your hearts are heavy with sorrow,
       sore with the grief
       not of our makings.
       But the Apostle lives,
       communes
       with our gods and ancestors....
       You have heard
       his predicament,
       heard the voice of despair,
       heard the voice of hope,
       seen the accursed messiah
       pining on our garbage heap
       mourning
       the unmourned heroes of the clan,
       the forgotten nationalists
       whose blood
       boils under our feet,

       all the undying heroes
       who, in protecting

the gem of fatherland
met hot death
on the keen edges of tyrant's knives....
*(Sustained blasts of thunder. Lunatic shudders, looks astonishingly
above his head. Pause.)*
I should be going.
The night is growing old
and the womb of the sky rumbles.
Who knows what monster it shall bear?
I have reached the end of the message
I carried in my womb
since the first peal of thunder
since my first dark dawn.
My heart is too grieved
that tongues cannot tell,
my lips too heavy to say more
and I must go now...
(Pause.) But remember,
go home and boil your herbs
fetch colanuts, palmwine, salt
swines, goats, *njieh, nkeng*...
go to Fuandem's shrine
and in a rite
weep in the nave till the rock trembles;
wail at ancestral graves
till old skulls smile with fractured teeth....
we might be safe again....
I must be going...
Farewell. *(Exits.)*

Fin

Ancestral Earth

Dramatis Personae

MAFUA:	A Leader of the Women of Allehtendurih
M'MEKA:	Another Leader of women
AKEUMBIN:	King of Allehtendurih
AFINGONG:	The King's Fiftieth bride
LEBU:	Prince of the Air
NTSE:	Prince of the Streams
ESEIH:	Prince of the Soil
M'MOK:	Prince of Fire
ALABI:	A Diviner and Priest of Fuandem
TROHNDI:	Chief Executioner

Other Executioners, Ancestral Voice, etc.

An opening in the sacred grove adjacent to the main entrance into the King's Palace. Far back, is a shrine roofed with thatches, the walls are made of barks of ancient trees. To the side, a short distance from the shrine, three men sit on wooden stools. A carved stool with the emblem of the lion and two others stand close to them. The men are dressed in simple traditional outfit, with sheathed machetes tied round their waists. They gaze in silence at something in the distance.

It is mid morning. Nguseng, king of the birds, sings in the sparsely-wooded grove. Noise of disgruntled women is heard in the background. MAFUA and M'MEKA enter. They stop at the threshold of the grove, a short distance away from the opening.

MAFUA: Here we have arrived
at the palace of Allehtendurih
where Akeumbin, our King,
the descendant of Anyankendong,
must tell us
if this Earth on which our feet stand
is the same in which our mothers
buried our umbilical cords.

M'MEKA: Mother Earth!
She no longer feels the keenness of our hoes.

MAFUA: And even when we scratch the soil into timid mounds
the crops laugh at our endeavours.

M'MEKA: Our skies are wide;
there are no clouds in the skies.
And the sun burns scourgingly on our backs
and brings us all the heat in the world.

MAFUA: Even now,
My twins are dead in my womb,
and the vomit of the living children is thin;
their stool is watery
like soup cooked by a mad woman.

M'MEKA: My own children are hungry; they are sick and pale

52

	like the spirit, my mother told me in a story,
	ferried wizards across the sky.
MAFUA:	The streams are sour; they are dry.
	We do not have water to drink,
	we can no longer fish the tadpoles
	and the crabs
	to pound *fufu* for our husbands.
M'MEKA:	And yet, our King, man beyond man,
	and our husbands
	do not scratch a pimple on their skins
	even when the soil
	continues to mock at our endeavours.
MAFUA:	*(Cynical laughter.)* M'meka,
	let me tell you a story.
	I harvested very few groundnuts and cocoyams last season.
	There wasn't anything to eat out of it.
	(Audible sigh.) I sold them to buy seedlings again this season.
	But my husband took the money
	to start paying the bride price of his new wife.
M'MEKA:	Ugh! These men!
	They don't feel how much we suffer
	to feed the home.
	Even when the soil frowns at us!
	My own husband! You will find him now
	in a *matango* house, drunk,
	with the little money he made
	from selling a deer he shot yesterday,
	the only animal he has shot
	after hunting for so many weeks.
	He didn't leave any *anini*
	in the house for children to eat.
MAFUA:	M'Meka, I am listening.
M'MEKA:	I tell you, Mafua.
	Yet he would complain of hunger,
	beat me and abuse my mother.

53

	He says my mother is from a bush tribe,
	the Yano tribe that produces palm oil.
MAFUA:	The men are all the same.
	We are dying, dying gradually with our children.
	But they don't care.
	They are in the *matango* houses drinking
	and waiting for food.
M'MEKA:	Mafua, shall we survive on this Earth for long?
	Shall we not wake from sleep one morning
	to find all of Allehtendurih dead?
	Like what happened in that far-away country
	they call "Anyos"?
MAFUA:	The Earth has changed its mind against us.
M'MEKA:	Yet, our husbands and
	the King sit like the stones
	that have nothing to do with hoes.
MAFUA:	We sent Alabi, the Priest of Fuandem,
	to beg the King to appease the Earth.
	The King never sent back kind words to us.
M'MEKA:	He must tell us today
	if this Earth which aches our feet
	is the same Earth our mothers used
	to praise in song *(Sings)*:

Mother, Mother Earth
Our wombs are fertile
Our crops are fertile
Our lives are fertile
Because your womb is fertile

We give back to your womb
The umbilical cord
Of your new-born child
Mother, Mother Earth
We live because you live *(Pause.)*

MAFUA:	M'meka, those were the days. *(Pause)*. We shall wait here at the entrance into the palace, till the King wakes from his young bride.
M'MEKA:	Fua Akeumbin! How he prizes Afingong! It is like he never knew a woman all his life, even though the palace is filled with women. Fifty in number!
MAFUA:	A man's appetite for women is like the appetite of the grave during a plague. Afingong is just taking her turn to feed the appetite of the King like others before her. She too will fade and the King will marry yet another wife.
M'MEKA:	But the King exaggerates with Afingong. See how much of the wealth of Allehtendurih is lavished on her, bangles, necklaces, cowries….
MAFUA:	She is still young and her blood is warm. The tender cocoyam leaf never knows that it will soon grow old and wither.
M'MEKA:	Mafua, let us go and wake up the King.
MAFUA:	No, let's be cautious. We will wait here till he wakes from sleep.
M'MEKA:	Mafua, three firestones can still throw away a pot. Let us meet him in his bed room. If he will not listen to us, then he should be prepared to marry all of us.
MAFUA:	M'meka, no. We will wait here. The King is our King no matter what happens. He is the father of our husbands. We shouldn't

	enter the palace as if
	we were waging a war against him.
	He will hear the noise and meet us.
	(In a low fugitive tone.) M'meka, See...,
	the Princes of the Earth are squatted
	under a shade in the grove.
	Are we safe where we stand?
M'MEKA:	Truly. There is something dreadful
	in the air that mouths are heavy to tell.
MAFUA:	*(Loud.)* We greet you, fathers of our children.
ESEIH:	Mafua, is it day break?
M'MEKA:	It is day break, Prince of the Soil.
ESEIH:	What brings you to the palace
	this early morning?
MAFUA:	We have come to see the King,
	Prince of the Soil.
LEBU:	This matter has teeth.
	See..., all the women of Allehtendurih
	have filled the palace courtyard.
MAFUA:	Prince of the Air,
	all the women of Allehtendurih could not
	come.
	But they will come
	if no one will listen to our grief.
M'MEKA:	The women present here are leaders of
	women's meetings and *njangi* groups.
LEBU:	Hmmm! Hmmm!
	I see something boiling in a calabash.
NTSE:	Crocodiles do not swim
	close to the banks of a river for nothing.
M'MOK:	Fire begins smouldering on fallen leaves,
	then it grabs the stem, reaches the branches
	and soon blazes above tree tops.
ESEIH:	When a flock of doves
	settles in a courtyard, never
	underestimate their purpose.
	Mafua, you are the leader of the women.

	Tell us: what monsters are you
	carrying in your wombs?
MAFUA:	Our children did not sleep in the night.
	They turned in their beds,
	cried, vomited and purged.
	And we have come to complain to the King.
M'MEKA:	Our children are dying
	and the King and our husbands are silent.
	The King and our husbands!
	Men, we thought, we were safe under their protection,
	men who should be ready at all times to
	unsheathe their machetes to fight
	when danger shows its ugly face....
MAFUA:	Men who should show us the right way
	when our fates
	are twisted and we don't know which
	road to take.
M'MEKA:	But our men....
	Gods of our ancestors! Our men are absent.
	We only see them when they shout at us
	to serve them food or when at night
	they force our limbs apart
	and tear us into pieces.
	Even last night while our children were choking
	and dying, our men
	still shamelessly hung tight to our loin cloths
	pulling us....
ESEIH:	That is not true M'meka.
	I too was witness of the night's terror.
	I saw my new-born child
	cringe with pain in my wife's arms,
	the only boy I have of eleven children.
NTSE:	The night was crammed with agony,
	with the groaning and crying of children.
LEBU:	Even the adults.

57

I am Prince of the Air,
but poisoned air aches my eyes,
my nose is heavy like a stone. *(Sneezes and coughs)*

ESEIH: My dominion is the soil.
From the beginning of times,
I have carried all the wonders of the Earth
on my bosom;
things living and unliving.
I am the hare that used to run
fastest in the forest.
But now, the forest runs fastest under my feet.
I have hunted the deer
for one whole season, and I did not see
any to shoot before it escaped.
The animals have abandoned my dominion.
And my heart is not on its seat.

NTSE: My region is in the streams, the lakes,
the springs, the ponds, the rivers....
From the beginning of life,
I was shaded by the forest.
I could see a cowry at the bottom
of the deepest lake.
I could see my image on the bosom of a pond;
and I would turn one side of my face
to the pond to admire,
and would see that it resembled my father's;
I turn the other side and it resembled my mother's.
But now, I cannot tell if this head I carry
on my shoulders is mine or someone else's
which has been struck by an evil spirit.

M'MOK: I am the Prince of fire.
I provide light to darkness
and give women the flames

58

to cook food for the family.
I provide warmth when it is cold
And heat the water with which kings bathe.
But I am misused.
Too many fires are burning on the
Earth and without good reason.
And my anger shall soon make me
roast the universe.

ESEIH: The soil is barren like a stone
that has nothing to do with a woman's hoe.
Trees have disappeared.
Even the Tree of Life....
See, there behind the shrine.... It bleeds....
The Tree of Life bleeds!
The oldest living witness of the land bleeds!
The very tree at whose feet
Anyankendong settled
when he led our ancestors from bondage to
the Earth of Allehtendurih.

NTSE: The trees that milked the streams
at the catchment have been killed.
And the lakes are muddy.
The Earth bleeds,
and the streams have the colour of an old
wound;
the water tastes like liquid from an old wound.
And when you drink,
your belly rumbles gbru gbru gbru like a
waterfall,
and all kinds of illnesses arrest you
at the instant.

LEBU: The sky is thin.
The air is heavy.
All the smoke of burning and toxic matter
have invaded the air;
all the smells of bad things stand stiff in the
air.

And there is little rain in the sky.
The sun lashes my balding head
And for many moons I have sneezed and coughed.
(Sneezes.) I am almost choking.

MAFUA: Prince of the Soil,
is it true that the King would not listen to Alabi?

ESEIH: You mean to appease the Earth
as our ancestors used to do?

MAFUA: Yes.

LEBU: The King has sworn upon Alabi's life.

MAFUA: Why?

LEBU: The King says instead that
Alabi and Afingong, the youngest of his fifty wives,
are cutting the ground under his feet.
Nothing would make the King think differently.

M'MEKA: *(Screams)* Wu-tuuuuuu!
Cutting the ground under his feet!
Gods of my ancestors,
Let the King not heap more curses on our heads!

LEBU: *(Prolonged sneeze)* The King has summoned
us this morning concerning the matter.
But our hearts are heavy.
Alabi has spoken as a seer.

M'MEKA: And that King!
His heart is always bitter
like the bile of the porcupine
when it concerns Afingong.
He prizes her more than all the women of Allehtendurih,
their mothers and their mothers' mothers
put together.

LEBU: And now... *(Sneezes)*

he wants to give Alabi the most terrifying
punishment in the land.

M'MEKA: *(Screams again)* Wu-tuuuuu!
Fuandem!
Does the bone no longer shield the marrow?
Would the King bring this terrible shame
to bear on the Priest of Fuandem
and cause more suffering in the land?

LEBU: *(Prolonged sneeze)* Alabi accuses
the King of causing general suffering.
He says the King has auctioned
the forests of Allehtendurih to strangers,
in exchange for a gun.

NTSE: The King and the Priest are like pork and fire.

MAFUA: Who is roasting who?

NTSE: Sometimes the King roasts the Priest,
At another time, the Priest roasts the King.

ESEIH: And the King is bent on persecuting Alabi.

MAFUA: *(Screaming.)* Wu eh eh eh eh!
What shall the children of Allehtendurih
tell their ancestors?

ESEIH: Does the squirrel no longer live in the tree?

NTSE: Does the crab no longer parade the bottom of
the stream?

LEBU: Does..., *(Prolonged sneeze)*, does the cloud
no longer settle on the shoulder of the
mountain?

MAFUA: Shall we stand on the hill top
like the cricket and call death to come and
take us?

NTSE: Does the thunder no longer announce
the coming of the rain?

MAFUA: Does the she-goat
no longer breast-feed the kid?
And even if the hen has no breast,
shall it no longer feed the chick
with the worms of the Earth?

61

Where shall we hide our faces in the Earth,
when our children, our children's children
shall come hurrying to the ancestral shrine,
crying of hunger and pain,
hitting our skulls and cursing:
"Mothers, wicked mothers!
Why did you deliver us to the bad side of life?
Why did you deliver us to a naked Earth?"
Fuandem, a terrible thing has happened
to Allehtendurih that mouths cannot speak!

M'MEKA: See..., the Son of the Lion comes,
accompanied by his cherished bride,
swaddled in the galore of necklaces
and bangles and earrings.

*Akeumbin enters the clearing in the sacred grove with Afingong.
Mafua and M'meka hail ululations as he enters. The King sits on
the Royal stool carved with the emblem of the lion. Afingong sits on
the other.*

ESEIH: *(Stoops and claps three times.)* Man beyond man,
may the light of the new day
make you live longer.

NTSE: *(Stoops and claps three times.)* Son of the Lion,
may your youngest bride
this day heal those ageing bones
that betray your limbs.

M'MOK: *(Stoops and claps three times.)* King beyond king,
may your day be warm and supple like dawn.

LEBU: *(Stoops and claps three times.)* Achiabieuh,
May this new day
bless you with ninety-nine senses
to tackle the problems of Allehtendurih.

AKEUMBIN: Yiieeuh! I thank you all.
May the new day bring you peace in your
homes. *(Pause.)*
Mafua, what brings you

and all the women of Allehtendurih
to the palace this early morning?
I could not sleep with the noise.

MAFUA: Father of our husbands,
we are old women of Allehtendurih.
We did not come to stir the Lion
from his beautiful bride.

M'MEKA: We came to tell the father of our husbands
that hunger and disease have invaded our
homes.

MAFUA: We can no more find the mushroom
that spread on the bosom of the Earth.

M'MEKA: Our soup tastes sour
and we can no more find the dry twigs to
gather,
even to heat our food.

MAFUA: The heat of the sun has brought our children
many fevers
and we can no more find the medicinal herbs
in our bushes
to squeeze into their eyes and nostrils.

M'MEKA: Even here, on this royal soil,
our feet do not feel the Earth on which they
stand.

AKEUMBIN: *(Sternly)* Go and till the soil,
you lazy women of Allehtendurih.
Your husbands are kind
else they should return you to your fathers
and ask the refund of the bride price.
I have, with my foreign friends, cut down the
forests,
and opened the land
so that you can work freely on the soil.
And you come here complaining
of hunger and disease instead of working?
Go and till the soil
before I tell your husbands

	what to do with you.
M'MEKA:	Nyatemeh! we can not move.
	Our feet are fastened to the root of this palace...,
	to the root of the Tree of Life
	that bleeds and we feel the pains.
MAFUA:	We till the soil every day
	from when the partridge
	sings praises to the morning
	to when the owl scares us at dusk with evil songs.
	But the soil mocks at us,
	and the crops grow sickly then wither.
AKEUMBIN:	Stand there then, and keep croaking
	like pregnant toads.
	(To the princes) You princes of the Earth,
	I summoned you here this morning to Lefem
	to execute the punishment of adultery
	on Alabi at the shrine of our ancestors.
	As tradition demands,
	whoever sleeps with the King's wife
	shall face the persecution of the broomstick.
	And this shall be done in the presence of Afingong
	my youngest wife
	whom he has destroyed with charms.
ESEIH:	Achiabieuh, we came at your request.
AKEUMBIN:	Alabi has been suspected of coveting my young bride.
	I have summoned the Trohndi
	to bring him here instantly for persecution.
	Aha! There they come.

Alabi is brought in by four executioners led by Trohndi. They wear gowns woven with raffia fibres which descend to their ankles and woven masks stuck with grass on their heads. They carry pikes, spears and other weapons of ancient warfare.

64

ALABI: *(Shouting)* Leave me alone, or I shall curse you.
MAFUA: *(Screaming.)* Wu-eh-eh-eh!
             Here comes the priest of Fuandem,
             flanked by the sons of Darkness.
M'MEKA: *(Weeping.)* Here comes the diviner of our lives.
             How shall we kill the snake
             that has coiled round our calabash of oil?
             Wu-t-u-u-u-u-! King of Kings,
             spare the disgrace on the priest. Let the
             diviner do his job,
             commune with our ancestors.
MAFUA: Father of our husbands, how do you give
             meat
             to a child and send a dog after him?
AKEUMBIN: Traitor, you have felt the young limbs of my
             virgin
             with witchcraft
             and now you have conspired
             with these croaking lazy women of
             Allehtendurih
             against me.
             Me, Akeumbin, son of the Lion!
             Descendant of Anyankendong!
             You conspire against me.
             Wizard, you shall die according to tradition.
ALABI: Do what you want to.
AKEUMBIN: And I must, slave.
             Trohndi, hold him firm before
             I pronounce my judgement.
             Princes of Allehtendurih, as I was saying,
             I summoned you this morning
             to be witness of a prosecution on charges of
             adultery.
             Alabi has used charms
             and witchcraft to seduce my youngest wife
             and he shall be persecuted in her presence

according to tradition.
I have consulted the ancestors
and his punishment is straightforward:
a broomstick shall be inserted and broken in
Alabi's maker-of-children.
And after, he shall be taken to the farthest
forest
and banished for life.

MAFUA: Break a broomstick in Alabi's maker-of-
children?
God of my ancestors!
Do not allow the fatal thought to bear.
Let the King not heap more curses on our
heads?

ALABI: Before you pursue your evil thoughts
you must first confess to the gods of the land
how roughly you have treated the Earth
to suckle your wild passions.

AKEUMBIN: Adulterer, you must die.

ALABI: Fua Akeumbin,
think of the poor women of Allehtendurih,
think of the children they shall bear
to live on this Earth in a world without end
and appease the ancestors. They have
abandoned the earth.

AKEUMBIN: I shall not.
I think I am doing Allehtendurih so much
good.
We had to put down the forest
to make the land bright,
so that anyone can see where he puts his leg.
The world is changing
so Allehtendurih must change too.
That is what the red people from
faraway land told me.
Do you not see how bright the land looks?
Answer me, adulterer.

	Even the Redman has abandoned his country and pleads to live here.
ALABI:	And so you have auctioned our Earth to strangers, destroyed the Tree of Life, and in compensation you were given a gun, and ornaments to dress your young wife.
AKEUMBIN:	Aha! have I not said it before? Have I not said that the viper's tongue is poisonous because it has no legs? I have told you this mad man wants my young bride. He shall die according to tradition.
ALABI:	Akeumbin, forget about your young bride, and think of the damage you have caused to the Earth of Allehtendurih.
AKEUMBIN:	I have done no harm.
ALABI:	Akeumbin, is this Earth the Earth of Allehtendurih which many seasons ago was the song of joyful and robust men, women and children?
AKEUMBIN:	Answer your charge first. Do not become the woman who goes to deliver but first gives birth to her womb
ALABI:	Akeumbin, is this the Earth, our ancestral Earth, which when we were young, pulsed with life?
AKEUMBIN:	Do not talk like a lunatic. Plead guilty of your charge.
ALABI:	I have no guilt to plead.
AKEUMBIN:	You are guilty of adultery, wizard.
ALABI:	Akeumbin, answer me straight. Is this Allehtendurih whose land was filled with the wealth of nations, on whose mountains

the leopard snarled with pride,
and the lion roared with verve in the jungle?

AKEUMBIN: This is a trick to escape persecution,
to talk like a lunatic.

ALABI: Akeumbin, is this the land whose springs and streams
pure and healthy,
flooded into antique rivers?

AKEUMBIN: Trohndi, make the adulterer impotent.

ALABI: Do not let your foolishness eat up your head
and heap more curses on the heads
of the children of Allehtendurih.

AKEUMBIN: Trohndi, where is the broomstick?

ALABI: The fields of Allehtendurih wither,
the mountains stand like a sore
in the eye of the sun, the streams dry up,
the air chokes
and the red strangers are there digging up things
only gods alone know
and carting them away to their country,
cutting down trees and destroying our totems
as if they have heard
the world was coming to an end so soon.
And the children of Allehtendurih are sick
they are dying, dying.
Akeumbin, I cannot feel
the warmth of Allehtendurih any more.
I cannot feel the warmth of this Earth any more.

AKEUMBIN: Trohndi, persecute him
before the partridge sings at mid day.

MAFUA: The partridge that used to sing in the woods
is heard no more.
Our shadows melt under our feet
when noon comes.
And we cannot say how old is the day.

M'MEKA: There is no life in the bushes...,
          even here in Lefem, there is no life.
          The many-coloured birds
          that twittered in the undergrowth,
          the young moles that raced through the Earth,
          the deer that dreamt all day under a shade
          chewing the cud,
          the leopard that walked with majesty
          from jungle to jungle
          and the lizard nodded with adoration
          from a crack in a tree....
          These and many other wonders
          on the bosom of the Earth are seen no more.

MAFUA: See...! See, the Tree of Life bleeds.
          Some one has cut its arms
          and it stands desolate in the sun....
          The Tree of Life that no one shall scratch.
          Woe to Allehtendurih!

AKEUMBIN: Trohndi, have you been hypnotised
          by those indolent women?
          What are you waiting for?

TROHNDI: Achiabieuh! I think....

AKEUMBIN: Get on him and stop thinking.

TROHNDI: Descendent of Anyakendong,
          I think the Priest speaks some truth....

AKEUMBIN: I say make him impotent
          or I will yank off your head.

TROHNDI: Father of the land....

AKEUMBIN: Do you speak still, instead of acting? *(Pause.)*
          Trohndi, are you not my Chief Executioner?
          Or, have the women bribed you with fufu?
          (Pause.)
          Who is there? Bring my gun!

TROHNDI: Your Highness, be patient and....

AKEUMBIN: Insert the broomstick
          before I lose my temper.
          What business have worms in matters that

69

	concern bones?
ALABI:	A ram has teeth, but it cannot eat the bone.
	It eats grass, Akeumbin.
AKEUMBIN:	Trohndi, I say insert the broomstick
	and do not stand there
	counting your teeth with your tongue, you traitor.
ALABI:	Akeumbin, you are the traitor
	to the children of Allehtendurih.
	You have sold their land because
	of greed and wickedness.
AKEUMBIN:	Slave, do you call me "traitor"?
	Do you know on which Earth you stand?
ALABI:	On the Earth of our ancestors
	and not that of Akeumbin.
AKEUMBIN:	You abuse me in front of the common women folk
	of Allehtendurih?
	In front of my young bride?
	Where is my gun? *(Pause. No one moves.)*
	Is no one stirring? *(Pause.)*
	Nkem Eseih! *(Pause)* Nkem Lebu! Bring my gun! *(Pause.)*
LEBU:	Nyatemeh, listen…, *(Prolonged sneeze.)*
AKEUMBIN:	Bring my gun and stop sneezing.
	Do you keep bees in your nostrils? *(Silence.)*
	Is no one moving? *(Rises and moves about angrily)*
	Hoii! Will no one move? Will no one answer? *(Silence.)* Answer me or
	I shall wrench off all your heads. *(Silence.)*
	Where is Nkem M'mok? *(Pause)* Nkem M'mok! *(Silence.)*
	Nkem Eseih! Nkem Lebu! Nkem Nntse! *(Silence.)*
	Has the wizard struck everyone here dumb?
	Is everyone deaf?
	I say bring my gun

else *Amoh* will strike all of you to death.
*(Pause then louder.)*My g-u-n!
(Rushes to Eseih and tries to unsheathe his machete. Eseih holds it firm to his waist. Akeumbin stands shocked and stares about, bewildered.)

MAFUA: The Son of the Lion shall not persecute
the disciple of truth.

M'MEKA: How can he persecute the Priest of Fuandem?

MAFUA: Let the King not heap more curses on our
heads.

M'MEKA: We are poor women of Allehtendurih.
Our children's husbands cannot build their
own houses,
they can not find the thatch to build their
huts.

MAFUA: Son of the Lion, save the children of
Allehtendurih
by doing what the Priest has said.

ESEIH: Nyatemeh,
calm down and listen to the cry of the people.

M'MOK: Achiabieuh, anger that burns like
wild fire soon smoulders in its own ashes.

LEBU: Your Majesty, listen to the cry of the women,
for in their wombs we become men.

(Akeumbin returns, sits and continues to stare wildly about)

NTSE: Tooth of the Elephant,
the eyes are in the head,
but they do not see the head in which they are
fixed.
King of Kings, listen to what your people say.

ESEIH: You have said everything,
prince of the rushing streams.

LEBU: You have spoken like a god,
Master of the mighty ponds.

AKEUMBIN: *(Turning slowly towards Afingong.)* Afingong!

AFINGONG: Your Majesty. *(She moves and stoops before
Akeumbin.)*

71

AKEUMBIN: Have I lost my head?

AFINGONG: No, Your Majesty.

AKEUMBIN: Then what am I doing here?

AFINGONG: The children of Allehtendurih want you to rescue them.

AKEUMBIN: How?

AFINGONG: They want you to appease the ancestors of the land
and forget about all accusations of any relationship
between the diviner and I.

AKEUMBIN: Do you mean that wizard has never spoken to you?

AFINGONG: Never, my husband.

AKEUMBIN: He has never felt your young limbs?

AFINGONG: Never.

AKEUMBIN: Never sailed between your milky thighs?

AFINGONG: Never, Your Majesty.

AKEUMBIN: Never dreamt of it? Never?

AFINGONG: Never, Your Majesty. I never could betray
my husband's most prized love for me.

AKEUMBIN: Never?

AFINGONG: Never, my husband. I am still the same
as you found me, and cropped me.
Father of my children, forget about me
and listen to the cry of my mothers.

AKEUMBIN: There is no question of listening to
queer old idle women. *(Grumbling of women.)*

AFINGONG: But they want you
to appease the ancestors, my husband.

AKEUMBIN: No!

AFINGONG: That is what they say.

AKEUMBIN: *(Rising vehemently.)* Who said it?
Call the person's name let him come forward
and confess his crime.
Shall anyone tell me, Akeumbin, what I
should

72

or should not do?
Let the Earth of Allehtendurih crumble
into some deep darkness
and leave me and my bride alone.
(The women hail a cry of denunciation.)
Stop croaking there, you pregnant toads.
(Another cry of denunciation.)
Afingong, tell me who said it. *(Silence.)*
Afingong, answer me!
Or are you too mad?
Have you connived with the wizard?
Where is my gun? *(Silence)*
I will shoot down all of you. My g-u-n! *(Pause.)*
Nkem Eseih! *(Pause.)* Nkem Lebu! *(Pause)*
Are not these faces I see around me? *(Loud)*
My g-u-n! *(Pause)*
Am I of any substance? Do I have flesh?
Bring my gun!
(Silence) No one is moving still?
Do they not hear the roar of the Lion?
Or am I deaf and dumb and could only hear
my own voice?
(Louder) My g-u-n!

ALABI: You have destroyed the jungle, Akeumbin
And so there can be no lions.

AKEUMBIN: What? Alabi, do you still live?
I shall go for the gun myself.
*(Rises, about to exit. Turns instead and grabs Alabi
on his neck.*
There is a brief scuffle.)
Adulterer? I will murder you with my hands.

AFINGONG: *(Rises and pulls Akeumbin to his royal stool.)*
Listen, Your Majesty
I feel a sharp pain in my womb.
If for my sake, you shall leave
my mothers and their children in pain and
agony

Then, I shall cut off these necklaces that sever me

from my umbilical cord,

and join my mothers in their misery

until you listen to their plea.

I too shall have children, Your Majesty.

(Cuts of the necklaces, throws them on the ground and crosses over to join the women.)

AKEUMBIN: Afingong, do not go anywhere.

Has Alabi charmed you at last? *(Pause.)*

Is she gone?

Afingong I shall quarter you into pieces

if you move another step.

(Loud.) A-f...i...ng...o...ng! *(Pause.)*

Shall no one answer the Lion?

Not even my echo returns to me?

ESEIH: Nyatemeh, there can be no echo in the desert.

The land is gone.

LEBU: Achiabieuh, do what the people want. See...,

Even your youngest bride is against you now.

AKEUMBIN: *(Still tottering about)* Have I been bewitched?

Is this Akeumbin?

Is this the voice that cried "Hoii!"

and princes trembled? Nkem Nste! Nkem Lebu! Nkem Eseih!

(Silence) See. They stare at me as though I was a shadow.

ESEIH: Nyatemeh, you are not a shadow.

AKEUMBIN: Then who am I?

ESEIH: You are our King, the custodian of our lives.

AKEUMBIN: I am a shadow, you cannot deceive me.

There is no substance in me

if the roar of the lion will not make a rat panic.

There is no substance in me.

(Falls first on knees, then lies prostrate on the earth, while the women and the men watch him. Long

silence.)
My ancestors,
I am the only mad man in Allehtendurih.
Anyankendong…Mbe   Tanju-Ngong,
Achenkeng…,
I have offended you beyond reproach.
Forgive me, children of Allehtendurih.
Forgive me fathers of the Earth.
We shall talk to you in the shrine just now.
(Rises, moves towards the ancestral shrine, opens and enters.
Alabi enters also, followed by the Princes of the Earth.)

MAFUA: We are happy, our King has conceded.
King of Kings, he has conceded,
a little too late but better than never.
There he enters in the shrine
where our ancestors' skulls
from the beginning of time are laid.
Alabi, the Priest of Fuandem with him.

ALABI: *(To the women.)* Sing Eseih and call back the ancestors to the shrine.
Someone should bring, salt, palm oil and *njieh*.

MAFUA: *(The women sing Eseih.)*
Fathers of our fathers
Wandering in the regions of the Earth
Return to your children

We offer this little salt
and a little palm oil to moisten the earth
Give us health, give us life.

AKEUMBIN: Hold on, women. *(Singing stops.)*
Alabi, talk to the fathers of the Earth.

ALABI: *(Sprinkling salt, palm oil and njieh round the skulls)*
Our ancestors,
accept our offerings of salt, palm oil and *njieh*
and greetings   from   the   children   of

Allehtendurih
as we uncover your skulls.
Anyankendong, you were the first
to settle on the foot of the Tree of Life,
the baobab that has seen life from the
beginning of times.
Mbe Nwet Ache-attah…, Mbe Tanju-
Ngong…, Achankeng…
all generations of our fathers and mothers
who live in the Earth.
We the children of Allehtendurih have come
to greet you.
We have come to tell you
that the Earth has abandoned us.
Our rich black Earth bleeds and we feel the
pains.
Pity us fathers
and bring us life again….
Princes of the Earth, talk to your fathers.

LEBU: *(Sprinkling salt, palm oil and njieh around the skulls)*
Gods of my fathers,
we have brought you our clean hearts.
We live as you showed us, humble and
prayerful.
Our lives are choking. Make us breathe again.
Give us plenty at harvest time,
give us peace, give us happiness, give us
healthy lives.
Give us children, water and air.

ESEIH: *(Sprinkling salt, palm oil and melon round the skulls)*
Mother Earth,
let your anger be softened with this oil.
Let this salt moisten the soil
and drive away the heat in the Earth.
Make the rains fall and crops grow.
Let us meet partridges on their eggs

And not the tigress on it cubs.
Give us abundant health till you call us
to live with you in the Earth.

AKEUMBIN: Gods of my ancestors, forgive me for my pride.
Let this oil soften your hearts
and make me rule Allehtendurih with the wisdom
of our ancestors.

There is a sound of the rushing wind. Sound fades. Ancestral Voice is heard from withal.

VOICE: Akeumbin, your greed and pride have made me shudder.
You do not resemble the colour of this Earth.
You invited red strangers
to barb the head of the Earth with a keen knife
and the children of Allehtendurih mourn.
And even when they mourn
you smear the Priest of Fuandem with lies and shame.
Akeumbin, what have you done to Allehtendurih?
Why have you wounded the heart of the Earth?

AKEUMBIN: God of my fathers, it was my own foolishness.
I had eyes and thought they could see my head.
Father, I accept my guilt.

VOICE: Women of Allehtendurih,
your tears have fallen in my heart
and I have tasted the saltiness of your fears
and agonies.

MAFUA: We are happy that our ancestors

	have felt our suffering.
VOICE:	Women of Allehtendurih, you too have ruined the Earth.
	You have burnt so many fires
	and given us too much heat in the Earth
	and we have wandered restlessly
	looking for another world to live in.
MAFUA:	God of our ancestors,
	we burned the thorny weed
	to hoe our farms and plant groundnuts.
VOICE:	Must you burn down a forest
	to plant a ridge of groundnuts?
	Women of Allehtendurih,
	why have you killed the nerves of the Earth?
	Have you not heard
	that mushrooms grow where the weeds get rot?
MAFUA:	Father of our mothers, we did not know what we did.
VOICE:	Prince of the Soil,
	you are the greatest of the Princes.
	You make the streams flow,
	you make the rains fall,
	you make the air light and pure.
	But you have hunted all the animals in the land,
	killed the antelope and its child to eat.
	What have you left on the Earth to multiply?
	Which animals shall your offspring see,
	taste and worship the wonders of the Earth?
ESEIH:	Father, we did not know what we were doing.
VOICE:	Besides, you have killed the raffia bush,
	the cassamango and the abobong trees,
	to plant the Redman's cocoa and coffee.
	The children of Allehtendurih need the milk
	of the raffia palm to make their limbs strong.
	They need the fruit of the wild trees

	that made them survive the fever.
	What have you left for the children of Allehtendurih?
MAFUA:	My ancestor, we were ignorant.
VOICE:	Listen, children of Allehtendurih.
	If you must chew a broken proverb,
	be careful with your tongue.
	The Earth is hungry.

The sound of the rushing wind is heard again, then it fades.

LEBU:	We have to make a heavy sacrifice
	to the gods of the Earth.
M'MEKA:	You speak the truth, Prince of Darkness.
ESEIH:	We shall make a great feast to feed the Earth.
	The Earth is hungry.
	We shall slaughter goats and pigs and chickens
	and offer to our gods. *(A very prolonged sneeze.)*
AKEUMBIN:	Children of Allehtendurih!
	I have put you in agony with my pride,
	my greed and foolishness.
	If a snake bites you, flee at the sight of a millipede.
	Let us be wise now.
	Our elders say that you do not feed a goat
	only on the day you want to
	take it to the market.
	The Gods of the Earth have spoken a lot
	and we don't yet understand.
	It is not the many goats and the pigs
	that you shall sacrifice on one day that matters.
	We shall feed the Earth in a different way.
	Go now, every one....
	With your children (any child who is old enough

to fetch a pipe for an old woman),
go with them and bring a seed,
a young plant or a stem that can be cut and
planted.
And this day of the week
shall henceforth be named LIUKSEIH,
a day all the sons and daughters of
Allehtendurih
shall feed the Earth with seed, plant and stem.
And we shall plant them all over
the barren lands of Allehtendurih.
Go now.

Everyone leaves the scene and returns immediately with seed, plant and stem. They sing and dance around the ancestral shrine still carrying the seed, plant and stem, while Alabi throws salt and palm oil and njieh on the ancestral skulls.

(Song)

Ancestral Earth
We shall care for you
and you shall care for us
give us plenty at harvest time
give us water, air and health
give us children, give us peace
Mother Earth,
the earth of our ancestors!
We live because you live.

Led by Akeumbin, everyone places the seedlings at the foot of the shrine. They sing and dance round, collect the plants and leave the scene in a procession, song and dance.

ACT DROPS